SpringerBriefs in Cybersecurity

W0193303

Cybersecurity is a difficult and complex field. The technical, political and legal questions surrounding it are complicated, often stretching a spectrum of diverse technologies, varying legal bodies, different political ideas and responsibilities. Cybersecurity is intrinsically interdisciplinary, and most activities in one field immediately affect the others. Technologies and techniques, strategies and tactics, motives and ideologies, rules and laws, institutions and industries, power and money—all of these topics have a role to play in cybersecurity, and all of these are tightly interwoven.

The SpringerBriefs in Cybersecurity series is comprised of two types of briefs: topic- and country-specific briefs. Topic-specific briefs strive to provide a comprehensive coverage of the whole range of topics surrounding cybersecurity, combining whenever possible legal, ethical, social, political and technical issues. Authors with diverse backgrounds explain their motivation, their mindset, and their approach to the topic, to illuminate its theoretical foundations, the practical nuts and bolts and its past, present and future. Country-specific briefs cover national perceptions and strategies, with officials and national authorities explaining the background, the leading thoughts and interests behind the official statements, to foster a more informed international dialogue.

More information about this series at http://www.springer.com/series/10634

Sophie Stalla-Bourdillon · Joshua Phillips
Mark D. Ryan

Privacy vs. Security

 Springer

Sophie Stalla-Bourdillon
Southampton Law School
University of Southampton
Southampton
UK

Joshua Phillips
Mark D. Ryan
School of Computer Science
University of Birmingham
Birmingham
UK

ISSN 2193-973X   ISSN 2193-9748 (electronic)
ISBN 978-1-4471-6529-3 ISBN 978-1-4471-6530-9 (eBook)
DOI 10.1007/978-1-4471-6530-9

Library of Congress Control Number: 2014943500

Springer London Heidelberg New York Dordrecht

Printed on acid-free paper

Springer is part of Springer Science+Business Media (www.springer.com)

Foreword

Securing privacy in the current environment is one of the grand challenges of today's democracies. While privacy is recognized as a fundamental right of individuals, and the right to privacy is enshrined in laws and constitutions, never before has privacy come under such serious, if not fatal, attacks as in the last few years. This is the result of two broad developments. First, technology is now available (and is routinely used) to entice, collect, store, analyze, and correlate massive quantities of personal data about individuals. The widespread adoption of cloud services and advances in big data techniques from commercial companies have enabled a series of new compelling and useful services (e.g., recommendation services, social networking, targeted advertisement, smart metering), but, at the same time, they have also made possible intrusions into individuals' private sphere on a massive scale. Second, privacy can be abused to hide illegal or threatening behaviors (for example, terrorism attacks). When faced with the choice of security or privacy, governments have increasingly chosen to forego privacy; in fact, as Snowden's revelations have shown, they have obtained broader permissions to engage in large-scale surveillance, in which privacy limitations are eroded in the name of national security.

This Brief in Cybersecurity explores the issues of privacy and security, and their complicated interplay, from a legal and a technical point of view. More precisely, Sophie Stalla-Bourdillon's chapter gives a thorough account of the legal underpinnings of the European approach to privacy, and examines their implementation through the privacy law, data protection law, and data retention law. In particular, it highlights where and how privacy protection breaks down to give way to other (conflicting) concerns, primarily that of security. The chapter by Joshua Philips and Mark D. Ryan focuses instead on the technological aspects of privacy and, in particular, on today's attacks on privacy, determined both by the simple use of today's technology, like web services and e-payment technologies, and by State-level surveillance activities. It also proposes "verifiable surveillance" (a way to make surveillance infringements of privacy quantifiable and verifiable) as a way to reconcile, by technical means, the need of a modern society to both defend privacy and allow well-defined breaches of privacy rights (e.g., for investigations).

It is interesting to observe that the challenges identified by these two chapters suggest that technology and legal instruments in isolation may not be sufficient to protect and put appropriate limits to privacy: technology and legal discourse need one another to draw reasonable lines and erect effective barriers around privacy. We hope this Brief provides a valuable step in this direction.

Marco Cova

Contents

Chapter 1
Privacy Versus Security...
Are We Done Yet?

Sophie Stalla-Bourdillon

> *"So, we're done. Welcome to a world where Google knows exactly what sort of porn you all like, and more about your interests than your spouse does. Welcome to a world where your cell phone company knows exactly where you are all the time. Welcome to the end of private conversations, because increasingly your conversations are conducted by e-mail, text, or social networking sites.*
> *And welcome to a world where all of this, and everything else that you do or is done on a computer, is saved, correlated, studied, passed around from company to company without your knowledge or consent; and where the government accesses it at will without a warrant".*
> —Bruce Schneier CNN March 16, 2013 (Bruce Schneier, The Internet is a surveillance state, March 16, 2013, available at http://edition.cnn.com/2013/03/16/opinion/schneier-internet-surveillance.)

Abstract It is often assumed that privacy and security are alternative values, which cannot be pursued together. Hence, the strength of the "nothing-to-hide argument": if you have nothing to hide, you have nothing to fear. Besides, ensuring the security of the network itself is said to actually require a detailed analysis of network flows. Reasonable expectations of privacy should thus progressively disappear in cyberspace. While it is true that enforcement of legal rules is a real challenge when communications are transmitted through the means of a borderless network, the evolution of the case law of the European Court of Human Right recently followed by the Court of Justice of the European Union does show that the right to respect for private life should have important implications online and in particular should significantly restrict the systematic collection and retention of content and traffic data by both public and private actors such as Internet service providers. At a time at which data-gathering and data-matching technologies are more sophisticated than ever, as illustrated by Snowden's revelations, it is crucial to fully comprehend the interaction between the protection of privacy and the furtherance of security in order to set appropriate limits to surveillance practices. The purpose of this chapter is therefore twofold: first, to shed light upon the European

© The Author(s) 2014

S. Stalla-Bourdillon et al., *Privacy vs. Security*, SpringerBriefs in Cybersecurity,
DOI 10.1007/978-1-4471-6530-9_1

approach to privacy and explain the interplay between privacy law, data protection law and data retention law; second, to explain how the values of privacy and security should be balanced together and in particular how privacy law should serve to scrutinise the appropriateness of measures implemented to ensure the security of the social group at large.

1.1 Introduction

One of my friends came home on a Sunday afternoon at about 3 p.m. While parking in a supposedly nice and quiet neighbourhood, two cars were waiting behind him for he was blocking the traffic. When he finished his parallel parking, the two cars stopped a few metres further. Something had happened while they were waiting behind my friend's car, but my friend could not really tell what. This is when the driver of the first car went out of his with a baseball bat and in a fury run to the second car and began to beat the car, the front glass, the back glass and then opened the door and continued to beat inside the car. The driver of the second car survived but ended up in hospital with very severe physical injuries. My friend was the only witness. He had called the police who arrived a few minutes after the leaving of the first car. My friend was able to give them the number on the license plate. He was then asked to give a statement to the police. This was the first time my friend had ever witnessed such violence and he was thus really concerned about the possible revenge of the assaulter. Besides, he learned afterwards that the assaulter was a recidivist. He was therefore willing to give a statement to the police as long as his name was not communicated to the defence. Yet, this was not an option available. "Do not worry" said the police officer, "even if we give your name to the defence they will not get your personal details and your address. They will not know who you are. And if you have to appear before a court we will put you behind curtains". And this is what he thought. "I have an unusual name. If the police give my name to the defence the accused will have no difficulty finding me through the means of the Internet. In fact he will have no difficulty finding where I live, where I work and how I look like. If for any reason he decides to take revenge and go after me nothing will stop him".

My friend was thus caught in a dilemma: to render the streets of the neighbourhood more secure radical measures had to be taken against the accused. And this would require him to give a statement to the police and eventually to appear in court. Yet by giving a statement he was agreeing to communicate his name to the defence, which would have had the consequence of putting him in danger, for the accused would then be able to locate him and his family very easily.

What this example shows is at least three things, if not four. First, it demonstrates that in some cases, not to say in many cases, privacy is a concern but not so much in the sense of being able to live or stay in a secluded place away from the public's eyes. What worries people is the subsequent use or misuse of personal information including personal information publicly available. Yet to prevent misuse of personal data, the most efficient way is to minimise the amount of data collected in the first place.

Second, security measures (aimed at the security of the society or of a portion of it) can be equivocal in terms of their impact upon the situation of its members if a comprehensive consequentialist approach is not adopted. In our example, asking testimonies to give statement to the police in order to put criminals in jail can have the consequence of jeopardising the well-being of the testimonies themselves and thereby can impact upon their own security.

Third, for security measures to be truly effective they often require going hand in hand with privacy measures. Indeed contrary to the common belief according to which one has to forego privacy protection in order to increase the level of security within the environment one interacts, in many instances ensuring the protection of private and/or personal data will help to render the environment more secure. This is true both offline and online, whatever the mode of interaction adopted.

One could counter-argue that there was a way to avoid such a dilemma: to install CCTV cameras[1] in the streets, and thereby collect and store personal data on a massive scale. In this way, the prosecution of criminals could have proceeded without human testimonies. Given the impulsive character of the assaulter, it is unlikely that the CCTV cameras would have prevented the assault in the first place. However, assuming CCTV cameras do enable police officers to identify individuals operating in the streets, then yes, my friend could have come back home without having had to give a statement to the police. This said, at this stage, several questions need to be asked. Do CCTV cameras ease identification of criminals and to which extent? On which scale should they be implemented to really ease identification? Are the data kept secure? For how long are the data stored? Who supervises the implementation process? Do individuals have a right to access the data stored? Are less intrusive technologies available? Are we better off with CCTV cameras everywhere in the streets or with a rule that would seek to allay witnesses' fear by allowing judges to adopt special measures within the courtroom and outside the courtroom and, for example, make it possible to take down critical content from the web to prevent witnesses' identification in some cases?

After the events of the 9/11 in the United States,[2] security programmes have been adopted at the national level to attempt to react in an effective way upon the terrorist threat. Up until the revelations of Edward Snowden, the most famous was probably the Total Information Awareness programme[3] implemented in 2003 but subsequently renamed the Terrorism Information Awareness Program after a public outcry denouncing the use of mass surveillance techniques.[4] More than 10 years after the events wide-ranging information-gathering capabilities are still

---

[1] CCTV stands for closed-circuit television as opposed to broadcast television. CCTV cameras are set up to transmit signals to a restricted number of monitors.

[2] Several authors have, however, showed that the security trend had initiated before the 9/11 events. See, for example, Lyon [1], Seamon and Gardner [2] at 372, Schulhofer [3].

[3] A data mining programme meant to track terrorists.

[4] Not to mention Operation TIPS standing for Terrorism Information and Prevention System, conceived as a domestic intelligence-gathering programme to have US workers having access to people's home report about suspicious activities. Operation TIPS was, however, abandoned after becoming known to the public.

considered a must-have as the UK Draft Communications Data Bill shows it, as well as the PRISM and Tempora scandals.[5]

In his recent editorial for CNN, Bruce Schneier[6] explains that protecting privacy interests on the Internet "is nearly impossible".[7] "If you forget even once to enable your protections, or click on the wrong link, or type the wrong thing, and you've permanently attached your name to whatever anonymous service you're using. Monsegur slipped up once, and the FBI got him. If the director of the CIA can't maintain his privacy on the Internet, we've got no hope".[8]

This impossibility to protect privacy interests he further explains is largely due to the grouping of two sorts of power: private power in the form of multinational companies such as Google, Apple and Facebook and public power in the form of law-enforcement agencies. Internet and online service providers generate a huge amount of data relating to users and a large number of public authorities are entitled to get access to these data and use these data.[9] At the same time, several private actors regularly use data produced by the governments themselves.[10]

---

[5] The PRISM/Tempora scandal generated public outcry after former CIA technical assistant Edward Snowden published secret US Government programme aiming at monitoring online communications conducted by the US National Security Agency. The first document published by the Guardian was a secret court order allowing the NSA to collect the telephone records of millions of US customers of Verizon, a big US telecoms provider. It then became clear that other methods of data collection were being used such as methods of upstream collection by tapping into fibre-optic cables and methods of downstream collection by being granted access to the servers of US Internet companies such as Google, Facebook, Apple and Yahoo. Huge amount of data are at stake since most of the communications of the world pass by the USA. The Snowden documents also revealed the existence of Tempora, a programme set up by the UK Government Communications Headquarters (GCHQ) in 2011 to collect data relating to phone and Internet traffic by once again tapping into fibre-optic cables. The GCHQ and the NSA were described as collaborating together. The Snowden documents also show that USA and UK intelligence agencies have managed to successfully weaken much of online encryption. The legality of these programmes with the European Convention on Human Rights has been attacked by Big Brother Watch, Open Rights Group and English PEN, together with a German Internet "hacktivist" and academic Constanze Kurz who have decided to present their case before the ECtHR. In the UK, Privacy International has filed two cases against GCHQ: in relation to mass surveillance programmes Tempora, Prism and Upstream, and the second in relation to the use by GCHQ of computer intrusion capabilities and spyware. See e.g. the statements of grounds submitted before the Investigatory Powers Tribunal by Privacy International on 8 July 2013, https://www.privacyinternational.org/sites/privacyinternational.org/files/downloads/press-releases/privacy_international_ipt_grounds.pdf. They have been followed by 7 ISPs who have also filled a complaint against GCHQ for the attacks allegedly run on the network.

[6] Schneier [5] (Schneier).

[7] Schneier.

[8] Schneier.

[9] See, for example, in the UK the long list to be found in The Regulation of Investigatory Powers (Communications Data) Order 2010 No. 480, available at http://www.legislation.gov.uk/uksi/2010/480/made.

[10] The Regulation of Investigatory Powers (Communications Data) Order 2010 No. 480.

Even though the collusion of these two types of power has been accelerated by the events of the 9/11, it would certainly have happened anyway. Indeed given the amount of data generated by Internet and online service providers and the automation of matching techniques, nothing is more tempting for both private and public actors to make use of them.

The easiest way to justify such data-gathering activities is to resort to the old value of security and argue that if one takes the security of the society as a whole, or more recently the security of the network, seriously one has to forego one's privacy.

Yet, this is oversimplifying, to an extreme, the terms of the debate and the balancing between two values that are far from being always in conflict.

At a time at which data-gathering and data-matching technologies are more sophisticated than ever, it is crucial to fully comprehend the interaction between the protection of privacy and the furtherance of security in order to attempt to set appropriate limits to these activities. The purpose of this chapter is thus twofold:

- First, to shed light upon the European approach to privacy and explain the interplay between privacy law, data protection law and data retention law.
- Second, to explain how the values of privacy and security should be balanced together and in particular how privacy law should serve to scrutinise the appropriateness of measures taken to ensure the security of the social group at stake.

In the next section, I will therefore give an overview of the evolution of privacy law from the invocation of the right to be let alone to the recognition of the right to respect for private life in Article 8 of the European Convention on Human Rights (ECHR). I will then expound upon the interplay between "traditional" privacy law which finds its roots in Article 8 of the ECHR and European data protection law. In the following section, I will consider data retention measures and see how they contravene the rationale underlying Article 8 of the ECHR, although this contradiction is already built within data protection law. Finally, I will focus upon the opposition between privacy and security with an intention to show that in most cases privacy and security go hand in hand and that assuming we are serious about both privacy and security, security measures relying upon the processing of personal data should be scrutinised through the means of a threefold proportionality test. First, the person responsible for the implementation of the security measure should establish that the measure will indeed increase the level of security. Second, she should demonstrate that no other less costly alternatives are available. Third, if the processing is highly invasive (i.e. implying the systematic collection and storage of personal data either by means of mass surveillance measures or targeted surveillance measures or the collection of sensitive personal data), competent public authorities should at some point address the question whether the processing at stake is at all needed in a democratic society irrespective of the consent given by data subjects.

1.2 Privacy Law

Privacy is an ever evolving concept.[11] In the legal field, its first express recognition can be dated back to the article of two prominent US lawyers Warren and Brandeis who coined the famous "right to be let alone".[12] Despite cross-Atlantic influences, the notion of private life has nonetheless developed in a relatively autonomous manner under the auspices of the European Court of Human Rights (ECtHR), which explains in part the more progressive stance of Europeans when it comes to the protection of privacy interests, at least on paper.

1.2.1 The Right to Be Let Alone

Warren and Brandeis were probably ones of the first to advocate the recognition of a right to privacy among legal commentators.[13] Writing at the end of the nineteenth century, they conceived the "right to be left alone" as a necessary instrument to fight against the "evil of invasion of privacy by the newspapers" [7]. The concern of Warren and Brandeis was in these years to find a legal institution that would have allowed individuals to protect themselves from intrusions upon the domestic sphere and in particular intrusions committed by the press. They comprehended the right to privacy as an extension of the right of authors to divulge their works grounded not on a traditional right of property but on a right to one's personality expressed in the following way. Everyone, they said, had a right to an inviolate personality and thereby should be entitled to prevent others from intruding upon their domestic spheres and subsequently divulge information gathered while illegitimately being in these secluded places.[14]

Interestingly, the first US doctrinal expression of a right to privacy is thus tainted with reflections influenced by the continental theory of personality rights developing at that time. This is accepted by Neil Richards and Daniel Solove who opine that Warren and Brandeis did not invent a new legal institution but have tried to shift "the conceptual underpinnings away from confidentiality toward what they called 'inviolate personality'" [14] in order to be able to grant individuals' remedies in case of injuries caused by the diffusion of new technologies, such as photo cameras, which allowed their owners to surreptitiously takes pictures of individuals in the absence of

---

[11] For a history of private life, see the 5 volumes edited by Philippe Ariès and Georges Duby, Histoire de la vie privée, Seuil, Univers Historique.

[12] Notably in France, for example, a few legislative provisions dealt with the protection of the secrecy of private life but in a very limited way. See Loi Relative á la Presse. 11 Mai 1868 and its Article 11 («Toute Publication dans un écrit périodique relative à un fait de la vie privé constitue une contravention punie d'un amende de cinq cent francs»). Riviére, Codes Francais et Lois Usuelles. App. Code Pen., p. 20.

[13] See nevertheless the comments of François Rigaux who recalls that in the UK, in France and Germany, several cases were already going in the direction advocated by Warren and Brandeis. Rigaux François [6].

[14] Warren and Brandeis at 214–218.

prior relationship existing between the parties. As these authors note, "Warren and Brandeis were not satisfied with confidentiality because they had in mind the candid photographer, a stranger who did not have a relationship with the subject of the photo. They observed that with earlier photographic technology, 'one's picture could seldom be taken without his consciously 'sitting' for the purpose".[15]

Warren and Brandeis went on to state that the right to be let alone should be recognised as a right against the world [7] and that "mere" injuries to feelings should give rise to a remedy. In this sense, these two authors were trying to build a bridge between the two "Western cultures of privacy" as highlighted later on by While James Whitman, the US tradition of liberty developed from the protection of the home and the European tradition of dignity developed from the protection of feelings [9].

But because underlying the right to be let alone as formulated by Warren and Brandeis was the fundamental distinction between the public and the private sphere, the remit of this sui generis right was ultimately limited. The right to privacy was deemed to cease "upon the publication of the facts by the individual, or with his consent".[16]

This is this right to be let alone as exposed by Warren and Brandies that has directly influenced the subsequent evolution of US tort law and in particular the formulation of a series of four tort actions designed to protect in one way or another privacy interests of individuals ultimately driven by the consolidating work undertaken by the famous tort law scholar Prosser: intrusion upon seclusion, public disclosure, false light and appropriation of name or likeness.[17]

In Europe, while some countries have never properly recognised privacy torts as such (i.e. the United Kingdom[18]) others have done so most often after the recognition of such a right by international instruments. This is the case of the French legislator who modified in 1970 Article 9 of the Civil Code[19] to add that every individual has the right to the respect of her private life.

By way of comparison, and before focusing upon the ECtHR case law, it is thus interesting to remark that although US tort law could seem generous towards victims of privacy violations, since even in the absence of "trusting" relationship between the parties a victim has a cause of action if she has suffered a moral injury produced by the publication of information considered to be highly offensive to a reasonable person, "[t]he American privacy torts have often struggled

---

[15] Richards and Solove at 132 citing Warren and Brandeis at 211.

[16] Warren and Brandeis at 218.

[17] See The American Law Institute, Restatement of the Law, Second, Torts, §652; William Prosser [10], William Prosser et al. [11]. Note that US privacy law is a composite body of law which comprises privacy torts and the fourth Amendment of the US Constitution. See the important ruling of the US Supreme Court in the case Riley v California 2014 WL 2864483 (U.S.Cal.) (it is now clear that a warrant is required for searches of cell phone data).

[18] See, e.g. Campbell v MGN Ltd [2004] UKHL 22 at [43]; Wainwright v Home Office [2003] UKHL 53 at [35] ("I would reject the invitation to declare that since at the latest 1950 there has been a previously unknown tort of invasion of privacy" per Lord Hoffmann).

[19] Loi n°70–643 du 17 juillet 1970—art. 22 JORF 19 juillet 1970.

when applied to the disclosure of personal data by businesses".[20] Underlying US tort law is the assumption that information that is public, including information that is transmitted to businesses, shall not be protected for the data subject cannot have any privacy expectations in such circumstances.

Generally speaking, such a difficulty can be explained by the prevalence of the secrecy paradigm which has had the consequence of significantly narrowing down the domain of the causes of actions arising from a violation of privacy interests.[21] This could be seen as the downside of the "success" of the right to be let alone.

One key question is whether in the era of the information society, differences between the Western cultures of privacy still persist today and whether the law-makers in Europe have been responsive to the challenges raised by the online world.

1.2.2   The Right to Respect for Private Life

The right to respect for private life to be found in Article 8 of ECHR encompasses two closely related prerogatives: the right to secrecy of private life and the right to liberty of private life. This dichotomy underlines the whole ECtHR's case law and in particular judgements dealing with surveillance measures broadly defined.

1.2.2.1   Secrecy and Liberty of Private Life

The ECHR[22] was signed on 4 November 1950 and entered into force on 3 September 1953. It is the second instrument after the Universal Declaration of Human Rights[23]

---

[20] Richards and Solove [8], at 176 (2007). See the US case U.S. West, Inc. v Federal Communications Commission, 182 F.3d 1224 (10th Cir. 1999) in which a telecommunications carrier criticized the privacy regulations of the Federal Communications Commission ("FCC") limiting the use and disclosure of customers' personal information in the absence of customers' consent. It was stated by the Court that: "A general level of discomfort from knowing that people can readily access information about us does not necessarily rise to the level of a substantial state interest, for it is not based on an identified harm. Our names, addresses, types of cars we own, and so on are not intimate facts about our existence, certainly not equivalent to our deeply held secrets or carefully guarded diary entries. In cyberspace, most of our relationships are more like business transactions than intimate interpersonal relationships". In Smith v Maryland, 442 U.S. 735 (1979), it had been held earlier that installation and use of a pen register (to record the numbers dialled on a telephone by monitoring the electrical impulses caused when the dial on the telephone is released) by a telephone company at the request of the police does not constitute a "search" within the meaning of the Fourth Amendment to the US Constitution.

[21] See, e.g. Solove [12], 497 ff (2006).

[22] Formally the Convention for the Protection of Human Rights and Fundamental Freedoms, Rome, 4.XI.1950. The Convention has been amended by several protocols.

[23] Text adopted by the General Assembly resolution 217 A (III) on 10 December 1948.

to recognise the protection of private life as a human right.[24] At the time of writing, 47 countries have ratified the Convention, Montenegro and Serbia being ones of the last entrants followed by Monaco.[25]

Notably, the drafters of Article 8 of the ECHR have adopted a broad expression—the right to respect for private life—although the ECHR was meant to encompass the minimum common denominators on which state parties could agree.[26] It is thus commonly presented as a more progressive instrument than the Universal Declaration on the Protection on Human Rights [13]. Article 8 reads as follows:

"Article 8—Right to respect for private and family life

1. Everyone has the right to respect for his private and family life, his home and his correspondence.
2. There shall be no interference by a public authority with the exercise of this right except such as is in accordance with the law and is necessary in a democratic society in the interests of national security, public safety or the economic well-being of the country, for the prevention of disorder or crime, for the protection of health or morals, or for the protection of the rights and freedoms of others".

The ECHR system relies upon the implementation of a (revolutionary at that time) right of individual petition, the right for natural and legal persons to sue their government before the ECtHR after having exhausted domestic remedies.[27] The ECtHR issues judgements that are binding upon the States parties to the Convention.[28] Because of its enforcement mechanism, the ECHR is often considered to be a very

---

[24] Other international instruments also include this right into their list of human rights: the International Covenant on Civil and Political Rights (art. 17) entered into force in 1976; the American Convention on Human Rights (Art. 11) entered into force in 1978; the New York Convention on the rights of the child (art. 16) entered into force in 1990.

[25] Montenegro and Serbia ratified the Convention in 2003, and Monaco ratified in 2004.

[26] Article 12 of the Universal Declaration of Human Rights is mainly concerned about illegitimate interference with private life. It reads as follows: "No one shall be subjected to arbitrary interference with his privacy, family, home or correspondence, nor to attacks upon his honour and reputation. Everyone has the right to the protection of the law against such interference or attacks".

[27] For quite some time, cases had first to be brought before the European Commission of Human Rights (established in 1954). If the case was deemed admissible, it would then proceed before the ECtHR. Initially, the European Commission of Human Rights was more a political body than a legal body. It was thus abolished by Protocol 11 (ETS No. 155) brought into force on 1 November 1998. The creation of a single Court was intended to prevent the overlapping of a certain amount of work, to avoid certain delays and to strengthen the judicial elements of the system. Other protocols have nonetheless followed such as Protocol 14 (Strasbourg, 13.V.2004).

[28] The Committee of Ministers of the Council of Europe, the Council of Europe's decision-making body, monitors the execution of judgements, to make sure in particular that damages are actually awarded to wining applicants.

successful experiment.[29] The ECtHR's case law thus constitutes the benchmark against which to assess the level of protection granted to nationals of the States parties to the Convention. "… [I]n order to find the rules of the English law of breach of confidence we now have to look in the jurisprudence of articles 8 and 10. Those articles are now not merely of persuasive or parallel effect … but the very content of the domestic tort that the English court has to enforce" said the English Court in McKennitt v Ash in 2006.[30]

This said, not everything is perfect obviously and commentators have complained about the intricacies of the ECtHR's case law. "[T]he Convention right to respect for private life is not easily understood. The right is ill-defined and amorphous"[31] say others. N. Moreham goes on stating that "[t]he breadth of the private life interest, combined with the Court's reluctance to identify either categories into which 'private life' can be divided or specific principles on which its decisions are based, makes it difficult to ascertain exactly what domestic courts should be taking into account when developing domestic law".[32]

It is nonetheless possible to identify at least two layers. The first one constitutes the core of the right to respect for private life and thereby the easiest to characterise, i.e. the delineation of a relatively secret sphere. The second one, in a way extending the borders of the first one, aims at enabling individuals to engage autonomously and freely with others. The distinction to draw is thus between secrecy of private life and liberty of private life.[33] "The right to respect for private life is not only the right to privacy, but also, to a certain extent, the right to establish and develop relationships with other human beings" stated the European Commission of Human Rights on the 18th of May 1976 in X v. Iceland.[34] Such a

---

[29] Note, however, that in some cases, the enforcement mechanism of ECHR rights remained for a long time ineffective. See the example of the United Kingdom. For many years, British citizens could not rely upon ECHR rights before national courts. In this sense, the ECHR was not a full part of British law. British citizens had to take a case to the ECtHR. Since coming into force on 2 October 2000 of the Human Rights Act, ECHR rights can now be asserted before national courts. More generally, see Sweet and Keller [14] and Sweet and Keller [15].

[30] [2007] 3 W.L.R. 194 at [11].

[31] See e.g. Moreham [16] (Moreham).

[32] Moreham at 45.

[33] This distinction has been used by authors such as François Rigaux, La vie privée, Une liberté parmi les autres, Larcier, Bruxelles, 1992 and Pierre Kayser, Protection de la vie privée, Economica, Paris, 2005 (Kayser). Interestingly, although Pierre Kayser acknowledges the usefulness of such a distinction right from the beginning, he decides to focus upon the protection of the secrecy of private life and not upon the protection of liberty of private life. This is the reason that he gives: «Nous n'envisagerons pas la protection de la liberté de la vie privée; qui soulève plus de difficultés encore parce que cette liberté consiste à la fois dans un principe et dans des libertés particulières s'exerçant dans cette partie de la vie, en particulier la liberté corporelle et la liberté de conscience» . Kayser n°62. In other words, because what Kayser calls the liberty of private life is intimately connected with the liberty of conscience, its scope and components are more difficult to identify. Besides, this author questions the fact that both dimensions of private life have the same ground. Kayser n°1.

[34] Application n°6825/74 (1976) 5 DR 86.

stance was then adopted by the ECtHR on the 16 December 1992[35] in the Niemietz case albeit with a different formulation: "[T]he scope of the right to respect for private life is such that it secures to the individual a sphere within which he can freely pursue the development and fulfilment of his personality".[36] While the Niemietz case still presents a dimension of secrecy worth of legal protection (the applicant alleged that the search of his law office constituted an unjustified interference with his private life and thereby a breach of Article 8), the fact that information gathered in commercial premises open to the public was protected shows that the ECtHR had been keen on adopting a broad interpretation of private life even before the boom of digital technologies.[37]

More recently, the ECtHR has been slightly more prolix: "...the concept of 'private life' is a broad term not susceptible to exhaustive definition. It covers the physical and psychological integrity of a person. The notion of personal autonomy is an important principle underlying the interpretation of its guarantees...The Article also protects a right to identity and personal development, and the right to establish relationship with other human beings and the outside world. It may include activities of a professional or business nature. There is, therefore, a zone of interaction of a person with others, even in a public context, which may fall within the scope of 'private life'. There are a number of elements relevant to a consideration of whether a person's private life is concerned in measures effected outside a person's home or private premises. In this connection, a person's reasonable expectations as to privacy may be a significant, though not necessarily conclusive, factor".[38]

While the protection of secrecy of private life echoes "the right to be let alone" as advocated by Warren and Brandeis at the end of the nineteenth century[39] paving the way to the tort of intrusion upon seclusion and public disclosure of private facts, the protection of liberty of private life clearly goes further. The protection of prisoners' correspondence exemplifies it. Some prisoners do not benefit from a right to keep their correspondence secret. However, in principle, these prisoners can exercise their right to liberty of private life whereby they are free to choose the recipient of their correspondence, unless legitimate limits are applicable in compliance with Article 8(2) of the ECHR.[40] When the ECtHR was asked quite early to interpret the right to respect for correspondence conceived as a component of the right to respect for private life, it therefore made it explicit that even if some individuals (prisoners in that

---

[35] Niemietz v Germany (A/251-B) (1993) 16 E.H.R.R. 97 (Niemietz).

[36] Niemietz, at [57].

[37] Niemietz, at [30]. However, Member States' leeway under Art. 8(2) "might well be more far-reaching where professional or business activities or premises were involved than would otherwise be the case". Niemietz at [31]. See also Reiss v Austria (1995) 20 E.H.R.R. CD90.

[38] Gillan and Quinton v United Kingdom (2010) 50 E.H.R.R. 45, at [61].

[39] Warren and Brandeis.

[40] See Campbell and Fell (1985) 7 E.H.R.R. 165; Boyle and Rice (1988) 10 E.H.R.R. 425; McCallum v United Kingdom (1991) 13 E.H.R.R. 597; Pfeifer and Plank v. Austria (1992) 14 E.H.R.R. 692; Peers v Greece (2001) 33 E.H.R.R. 51; AB v Netherlands (2003) 37 E.H.R.R. 48; Stojanovic v Serbia [2010] 1 Prison L.R. 286. See also Herczegfalvy v Austria (1993) 15 E.H.R.R. 437.

case) were not able to exercise their right to the secrecy of their correspondence they still could assert and exercise the right to the liberty of their correspondence.[41]

Before giving an overview of the range of privacy interests protected by the ECHR, it is crucial to begin by stating that the right to respect for private life has both a vertical and a horizontal dimension. In other words, not only do public authorities have a (negative) obligation not to interfere with the exercise of the right to respect for private life but they also have a (positive) obligation to make sure individuals are able to exercise their rights which implies when necessary "the adoption of measures designed to secure respect for private life even in the sphere of relations of individuals between themselves".[42] Because by definition, in cases of positive obligations, public authorities are not directly interfering with the exercise of the right to respect for private life of individuals, strictly speaking their abstention cannot be justified on the ground of Article 8(2). Article 8(1) investigation therefore becomes essential. Nevertheless the ECtHR's case law shows that Article 8(1) analysis is tied up with a balancing test echoing in fact that of Article 8(2).[43]

As aforementioned, there are different ways to articulate the case law of the ECtHR. One way of doing it is to distinguish between five categories of private interests: "[f]irst, there are the three 'freedoms from' rights (the first two of which correspond loosely with traditional private law conceptions of 'privacy')—the right to be free from interference with physical and psychological integrity, from unwanted access to and collection of information, and from serious environmental pollution. Then there are the 'freedoms to'—the right to be free to develop one's identity and to live one's life in the manner of one's choosing".[44] The problem with such a classification is that "freedoms from" and "freedoms to" overlap. As a result, the use of these categories does not really help to understand the outer limits of the right to respect for private life. This is true in particular when it comes to the regulation of surveillance. Yet if one adopts the secrecy/liberty distinction, one can distinguish between the collection, storage and disclosure of information meant to be retained secret and the collection, storage and re-diffusion of information publicly accessible. While both types of activities can amount to violation of Article 8(1), it should in principle be harder to justify the first category of interferences than the second category, as we are going to see. This is because we are moving from the core to the outer layer of private life.

---

[41] Silver v United Kingdom (A/161) 25 March 1983 (1983) 5 E.H.R.R. 347, at [86–104].

[42] Van Kück v Germany (2003) 37 E.H.R.R. 51 at [70]. See also Mosley v United Kingdom (2011) 53 E.H.R.R. 30 at [106]–[108], Von Hannover v Germany (2005) 40 E.H.R.R. 1 at [57]; Stubbings v United Kingdom (1997) 23 E.H.R.R. 213 at [60], McGinley and Egan v United Kingdom (1998) 27 E.H.R.R. 1 at [98]; X and Y v The Netherlands (1986) 8 E.H.R.R. 235 at [23] and Airey v Ireland (1979) 2 E.H.R.R. 305 at [32].

[43] Van Kück v Germany (2007) 37 E.H.R.R. 51 at [71]. See also Mosley v United Kingdom (2011) 53 E.H.R.R. 30 at [120], Karakó v Hungary (2011) 52 E.H.R.R. 36 at [19], Von Hannover (2005) 40 E.H.R.R. 1 at [57]; Rees v United Kingdom (1987) 9 E.H.R.R. 56 at [37]; Gaskin v United Kingdom (1989) 12 E.H.R.R. 36 at [42]; See also Hatton v United Kingdom (36022/97) (2003) 37 E.H.R.R. 28 at [119].

[44] Moreham [16] at 46 (2008).

"The notion of personal autonomy is an important principle underlying the interpretation of [Convention] guarantees",[45] explained the ECtHR in Pretty v United Kingdom in 2002. "[T]he very essence of the Convention is respect for human dignity and human freedoms"[46] added the ECtHR in the same case. The right to respect for private life is not an end in itself but a means to reach an upper objective: the protection of the right to human dignity. Human dignity is a broad umbrella. Violations of personal autonomy do not exhaust the category of violations of human dignity. To take an example, while imposing medical interventions against the will of a patient could be conceived as a violation of a right to one's personal autonomy and thereby one's human dignity for each individual should be able to choose how to be cured at least when it comes to cures of "minor importance",[47] searches on outsiders to the prison, who may very well be innocent of any wrongdoing, which are not undertaken in strict compliance with pre-determined safeguards can be conceived as amounting to a violation of a right to human dignity sanctionable on the ground of Article 8.[48] Indeed, there is a violation of the right to human dignity when the methods used to search are considered to be debasing. This is the reason why in the Wainwright case the ECtHR was able to find that "the application of such a highly invasive and potentially debasing procedure to persons who [were] not convicted prisoners or under reasonable suspicion of having committed a criminal offence must [have] been conducted with rigorous adherence to procedures and all due respect to their human dignity".[49]

The different layers of the right to respect for private life could thus be represented in the following manner (Fig. 1.1).

1.2.2.2   Surveillance and Private Life

Depending upon the way the category of individuals to be monitored is defined, one can distinguish between two broad types of surveillance: mass surveillance and

---

[45] Goodwin (2002) 35 E.H.R.R. 18 at [90] and I (2003) 36 E.H.R.R. 53 at [70]. See also R (On the Application of Perdy) v DPP [2009] UKHL 45 at [71] and [82], R (on the application of G) v Nottinghamshire Healthcare NHS Trust at [94], Pretty v United Kingdom (2002) 35 E.H.R.R. 1 at [61] and Van Kück v United Kingdom (2007) 37 E.H.R.R. 51 at [69].

[46] Pretty v United Kingdom (2002) 35 E.H.R.R. 1 at [65]. See also Wilkinson v Kitzinger [2006] EWHC 835 (Fam) at [11] and I v United Kingdom (2003) 36 E.H.R.R. 53 at [70].

[47] YF v Turkey (2004) 39 E.H.R.R. 34 at [33]. "On October 20, 1993, following her detention in police custody, Ms F was examined by a doctor, who reported that there were no signs of ill-treatment on her body. On the same day she was taken to a gynaecologist for a further examination. The police requested that the report should indicate whether she had had vaginal or anal intercourse while in custody. Despite her refusal, Ms F was forced by the police officers to undergo a gynaecological examination. The police officers remained on the premises while Ms F was examined behind a curtain. The doctor reported that the applicant's wife had not had any sexual intercourse in the days preceding the examination" [12]. See also MAK v United Kingdom (2010) 51 E.H.R.R. 14 and Storck v Germany (2006) 43 E.H.R.R. 6.

[48] Wainwright v United Kingdom (2007) 44 E.H.R.R. 40 at [47–48] (Wainwright). See also J Council v GU [2012] EWHC 3531 (COP).

[49] Wainwright at [44].

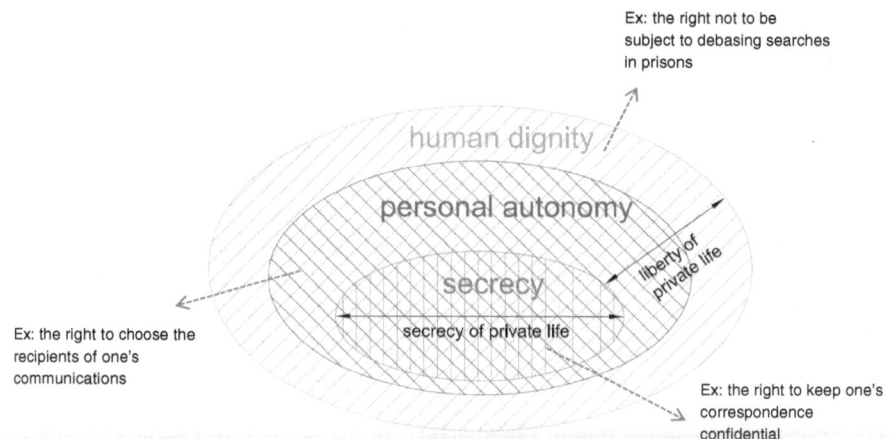

Fig. 1.1 The core and outer limits of the right to respect for private life

targeted surveillance. Mass surveillance, by definition "is not targeted on any particular individual but gathers images and information for possible future use. CCTV and databases are examples of mass surveillance".[50] Targeted surveillance concerns a lower number of individuals. "Targeted surveillance is surveillance directed at a particular individual and can involve the use of specific powers by authorised public agencies".[51] These are the definitions retained by the report drafted by the Select Committee on the Constitution of the House of Lords in 2009.

In 2006, the UK Information Commissioner commissioned the Surveillance Studies Network to compile a report on the surveillance society. The report published in November of this same year examined surveillance in everyday day life in the UK and its possible evolution in order to make recommendations as regards way to regulate it. As the UK Surveillance Studies Network wrote in 2006 "where we find purposeful, routine, systematic and focused attention paid to personal details, for the sake of control, entitlement, management, influence or protection, we are looking at surveillance".[52] Surveillance thus encompasses a wide range of activities which are not necessarily intrusive in the sense of implying an intrusion into a secret place. Indeed, the purposeful, routine, systematic and focused attention

---

[50] House of Lords, Select Committee on the Constitution, Surveillance: Citizens and the State, February 2009, available at http://www.publications.parliament.uk/pa/ld200809/ldselect/ldconst/18/18.pdf, p. 12 (HL Surveillance).

[51] HL Surveillance p. 12.

[52] A Report on the Surveillance Society, For the Information Commissioner by the Surveillance Studies Network, September 2006, available at http://www.google.co.uk/url?sa=t&rct=j&q=&esrc=s&source=web&cd=1&ved=0CCMQFjAA&url=http%3A%2F%2F;www.ico.gov.uk%2Fupload%2Fdocuments%2Flibrary%2Fdata_protection%2Fpractical_application%2Fsurveillance_society_full_report_2006.pdf&ei=nE5HUPP9MKjT0QXJvoCgBw&usg=AFQjCNE1m4QeMjz-U9CITqZMrG32meRykA, para 3.1. This definition is broad enough to include surveillance undertaken by public and private actors.

paid to personal details, even when these details are publicly accessible, can significantly hamper the exercise of the right to respect for private life.

Both mass surveillance and targeted surveillance measures amount to a prima
facie interference with the right of private life. The degree of seriousness of the
interference (i.e. whether the information is confidential, whether it is a preventive
measure targeting the mass of individuals) is relevant for the purposes of justifying
the measures. It is thus important to distinguish between different types of interferences in relation to the nature of the information collected, stored and eventually
misused. Four distinct categories thus emerge from the ECtHR's case law: interception of communications, monitoring of communications, collection and storage
of information relating to physical identity and collection and storage of information publicly accessible.[53]

Interception of Communications

D. Solove notes that, at least in the United States, in "many areas of law, the prevalence of the paradigm of secrecy has prevented the recognition of a certain number
of privacy violations".[54] In Europe, looking at the case law of the ECtHR, it is
manifest that a large number of decisions is concerned with violations to secrecy
of private life, rather than with violations to liberty of private life.

Is it to say that in Europe the narrow view of privacy has been prevailing as
well? Nothing is less sure at least if one looks at the ECtHR's case law.[55]
Although the boom of digital technologies has certainly made it harder to deline-
ate with clarity the contours of the right to respect for private life, as hinted above
the ECtHR has been keen on adopting and maintaining a broad interpretation of
that notion.[56] The right to respect for private life therefore includes "a zone of
interaction of a person with others, even in a public context".[57]

---

[53] Compare D. Solove taxonomy of privacy with the case law of the ECtHR. Solove [12] (Solove).

[54] Solove at 497. This author mentions the case of Nader v. General Motors Corp. 225 N.E.2d
765 (N.Y. 1970) (in particular at 768–771), in which General Motors had wiretapped Ralph
Nader's phone and extensively monitored his behaviour while being in public. Although the
Court acknowledged that in principle surveillance in public places cannot amount to an invasion
of privacy, in certain cases it may be "so 'overzealous' as to render it actionable". That being
said, surveillance could only be actionable to the extent concealed facts had been revealed as a
result of pervasive public monitoring. As a result surveillance in public places is not considered
to be illegitimate per se. See also Solove [17, 18].

[55] For a discussion about the strength of the secrecy paradigm in the UK see Stalla-Bourdillon,
Sophie (2011) Privacy is dead, long live privacy! Breach of confidence and information privacy:
towards a more progressive action for breach of confidence? In, Kierkegaard, Sylvia (ed.) Law
Across Nations: Governance, Policy & Statutes, IAITL.

[56] See in particular Peck v United Kingdom (2003) 36 E.H.R.R. 41 at [57]. See also PG and JH
v United Kingdom (App. No.44787/98), judgment of September 25, 2001 at [56].

[57] See for example, Gillan and Quinton v United Kingdom (2010) 50 E.H.R.R. 45 at [61],
Perry v United Kingdom (2004) 39 E.H.R.R. 3 at [36] and Von Hannover V Germany (2005) 40
E.H.R.R. 1 at [50].

With this said, surveillance, mass surveillance or targeted surveillance can be undertaken in different ways. The first one, the most obvious for the purposes of the regulation of privacy violations, is the interception of correspondences. Interception has been understood to cover "the obtaining of information about the contents of a communication by post or telephone without the consent of the parties involved".[58]

The increase in the frequency of telephone tapping in the 1970s and 1980s has given the ECtHR the occasion to issue a few judgments on the lawfulness of such investigatory methods. The seminal cases are Klass v Germany,[59] Kruslin v Fance[60] and Malone. Given the strength of the right to respect of correspondence, telephone tapping, in most cases, amounts to a violation of Article 8(1).[61] A fortiori when police installs specific devices in homes or business premises for the purpose of listening to individuals, these amounts to Article 8(1) breaches as well.[62] Even more, "[t]apping and other forms of interception of telephone conversations represent a serious interference with private life and correspondence".[63] It can, however, become legitimate if the conditions laid down in Article 8(2) are met. Telephone tapping is thus legitimate if it is done "in accordance with the law", if it pursues one or more of the legitimate aims referred to in paragraph (2) (i.e. national security, public safety or the economic well-being of the country, the prevention of disorder or crime, the protection of health or morals, or the protection of the rights and freedoms of others) and furthermore if it is "necessary in a democratic society".[64]

The requirement of being done "in accordance with the law" relies upon a two-fold examination. First, one has to determine whether there is indeed a legal basis

---

[58] Malone v United Kingdom Malone (1985) 7 E.H.R.R. 14 at [19] (Malone).

[59] (1979–80) 2 E.H.R.R. 214 (Klass).

[60] (1990) 12 E.H.R.R. 547 (Kruslin).

[61] Klass at [41]; Malone at [64]: "telephone conversations are covered by the notions of 'private life' and 'correspondence' within the meaning of Article 8". See also Huvig v France (1990) 12 E.H.R.R. 528 at [25].

[62] PG and JH v United Kingdom (2008) 46 E.H.R.R. 51 at [60]; Chalkley v United Kingdom (2003) 37 E.H.R.R. 30 at [24]; Lewis v United Kingdom (2004) 39 E.H.R.R. 9 at [18]; Elahi v United Kingdom (2007) 44 E.H.R.R. 30 at [17–18]; Hewitson v United Kingdom (2003) 37 E.H.R.R. 31 at [20]; Khan v United Kingdom (2001) 31 E.H.R.R. 45 at [25]; Armstrong v United Kingdom (2003) 36 E.H.R.R. 30 at [19]; Allan v United Kingdom (2003) 36 E.H.R.R. 12 at [35]; Wood v United Kingdom (App. No.23414/02), [2004] Po. L.R. 326 at [33].

[63] Kruslin at [33].

[64] A few exceptions to the right to respect of correspondence have been recognized by the ECtHR in particular in cases brought by prisoners. In Campbell v UK (1993) 15 E.H.R.R. 137 at [48]: "the prison authorities may open a letter from a lawyer to a prisoner when they have reasonable cause to believe that it contains an illicit enclosure which the normal means of detection have failed to disclose. The letter should, however, only be opened and should not be read. Suitable guarantees preventing the reading of the letter should be provided, e.g. opening the letter in the presence of the prisoner. The reading of a prisoner's mail to and from a lawyer, on the other hand, should only be permitted in exceptional circumstances when the authorities have reasonable cause to believe that the privilege is being abused in that the contents of the letter endanger prison security or the safety of others or are otherwise of a criminal nature. What may be regarded as 'reasonable cause' will depend on all the circumstances but it presupposes the existence of facts or information which would satisfy an objective observer that the privileged channel of communication was being abused".

within the national system on the ground of which the surveillance measure has been adopted. Second, one has to assess whether this legal basis is of quality, i.e. whether the legal basis is accessible and foreseeable.[65]

Foreseeability of the legal basis, as to the nature and effect of the surveillance measure, is a crucial condition which has been lacking in a series of cases. Building upon its decision rendered in the case Silver v. United Kingdom,[66] the ECtHR explained in Malone[67] how such a condition has to be interpreted in surveillance cases: "the requirement of foreseeability cannot mean that an individual should be enabled to foresee when the authorities are likely to intercept his communications so that he can adapt his conduct accordingly. Nevertheless, the law must be sufficiently clear in its terms to give citizens an adequate indication as to the circumstances in which and the conditions on which public authorities are empowered to resort to this secret and potentially dangerous interference with the right to respect for private life and correspondence".[68] Said otherwise "the law must indicate the scope of any such discretion conferred on the competent authorities and the manner of its exercise with sufficient clarity ... to give the individual adequate protection against arbitrary interference".[69]

The Kruslin case may be more telling than the Malone case. In Kruslin, the pre-existing legal framework was more comprehensive.[70] Legal rules, although imperfect, had been adopted to govern the issuance of warrants through the means of which judges could order the tapping of telephone lines. Notably, despite the presence of several safeguards (such as the need for a decision by an independent judicial authority, an investigating judge; the supervision of senior police officers; the possibility to appeal the decision of the investigating judge; the prohibition to resort to any 'subterfuge' or 'ruse' consisting not merely in the use of telephone tapping but in an actual trick, trap or provocation in order to tap communications; and the duty to respect the confidentiality of client-to-lawyer

---

[65] See, e.g. Malone at [67] ff; Kruslin at [27] ff.

[66] (1983) 5 E.H.R.R. 347. The ECtHR ruled that "a law which confers a discretion must indicate the scope of that discretion" at [88].

[67] In this case, the applicant, an antiques dealer, had been prosecuted for a number of offences relating to dishonest handling of stolen goods but then acquitted. During the trial, his telephone conversation had been intercepted and monitored on the authority of a warrant issued by the Secretary of State for the Home Department. After his acquittal, the applicant initiated some proceedings and claimed that the tapping of his telephone had been done in violation of Article 8.

[68] Malone at [67].

[69] Malone at [68].

[70] In Malone, there was no overall statutory code governing interceptions of communications, although various statutory provisions were applicable thereto. That being said, the bulk of the provisions at stake were mere "administrative" provisions coming from a Government's White Paper of 1980 entitled 'The Interception of Communications in Great Britain' presented to Parliament by the then Home Secretary in April 1980, Cmnd. 7873. Such administrative rules had no binding effects. Importantly, the law of England and Wales did not expressly require the issuance of a warrant for the purposes of exercising the power to intercept communications. As a result, "it cannot be said with any reasonable certainty what elements of the powers to intercept are incorporated in legal rules and what elements remain within the discretion of the executive". Malone at [79].

relationships[71]) the ECtHR held that the French legal basis was not foreseeable. According to the ECtHR "[a]bove all, the system [did] not for the time being afford adequate safeguards against various possible abuses. For example, the categories of people liable to have their telephones tapped by judicial order and the nature of the offences which [might have given] rise to such an order [were] nowhere defined. Nothing [obliged] a judge to set a limit on the duration of telephone tapping. Similarly unspecified [were] the procedure for drawing up the summary reports containing intercepted conversations; the precautions to be taken in order to communicate the recordings intact and in their entirety for possible inspection by the judge (who [could] hardly verify the number and length of the original tapes on the spot) and by the defence; and the circumstances in which recordings may or must [have been] erased or the tapes [been] destroyed, in particular where an accused [had] been discharged by an investigating judge or acquitted by a court".[72]

As a result, it does seem crucial to be able to sufficiently identify in advance the categories of people[73] who could have their phone lines tapped and the nature of the offences which may give rise to such an order. This should have the implication that such invasive practices should only be used in exceptional cases, to target a limited number of individuals, in order to prevent or react upon the commission of serious offences.

The foregoing conclusion seems to be confirmed by Klass. In this case, the German provisions under scrutiny did identify with a relative high degree of precision the category of persons to be listened to. Not unsurprisingly the ECtHR had nothing to criticise. Among the different safeguards set forth by the German provisions, one could find the following one: the surveillance could cover only "the suspect or such other persons who [were], on the basis of clear facts (bestimmte Tatsachen), to be presumed to receive or forward communications intended for the suspect or emanating from him or whose telephone the suspect [was] to be presumed to use".[74] Not only were "factual indications for suspecting a person of planning, committing or having committed certain serious criminal acts"[75] necessary to render the surveillance legitimate, but also the assurance that "the surveillance [could] cover only the specific suspect or his presumed 'contact-persons'".[76] Remarkably for our purpose, the ECtHR stressed that "so-called exploratory or general surveillance [was] not permitted by the contested legislation".[77]

As a result, the ECtHR was able to hold that it was satisfied that there existed adequate and effective guarantees against abuse. There was thus ultimately no

---

[71] Kruslin at [34].

[72] Kruslin at [35].

[73] But obviously not each individual belonging to this category.

[74] Klass at [16].

[75] Klass at [51].

[76] Klass at [51].

[77] Klass at [51].

breach of Article 8[78] even though in most cases individuals who had been under surveillance were not informed about the fact that they had been indeed listened to.[79] The setting up of control mechanisms to ensure the performance of the surveillance complied with applicable legal norms and the rule of the law appeared to be enough. Interestingly, in the case at hand, although judicial control had been excluded, the ECtHR nevertheless concluded that the control mechanisms made the interception a proportionate interference.[80] Such a conclusion had been reached probably because Klass was a national security case and therefore an exception. Indeed in most cases, the principle had to be the following: "[t]he rule of law implies, inter alia, that an interference by the executive authorities with an individual's rights should be subject to an effective control which should normally be assured by the judiciary, at least in the last resort, judicial control offering the best guarantees of independence, impartiality and a proper procedure".[81]

More than 10 years later, it does seem that the lessons of the Malone case have been (partially) learnt by the UK legislator.[82] In Kennedy v UK,[83] the applicant, who had been convicted in 1994 of manslaughter and sentenced to 9 years' imprisonment, alleged that his communications (mail, telephone and emails) had been intercepted in violation of Article 8, in order to intimidate him and undermine the business activities he had started after having been active in campaigning against miscarriages of justice. He also alleged that the UK Regulation of Investigatory Powers Act 2000 (RIPA 2000) was not a satisfactory legal basis for the purposes of Article 8(2). The ECtHR found that it could not "be excluded that secret surveillance measures were applied to the applicant or that he was at the material time, potentially at risk of being subjected to such measures".[84] Therefore, the Court had to check whether the interference could be justified under Art. 8(2). However, the Court held that the interference was justified. The ECtHR examined both RIPA 2000 and its Code of Practice (The Interception of Communications Code of Practice) to find that the nature of the offences which could give rise to an interception was sufficiently clear[85] (and in particular the terms "national secu-

---

[78] Klass at [60].

[79] The reason given to justify such a solution was that not informing individuals who had been under surveillance was necessary to ensure the efficacy of the interception. Klass at [58].

[80] Klass at [56]. Judicial review had been replaced by a two-tiered system: first an official qualified for judicial office would review the implementation of the surveillance measure and make sure only relevant information was kept. At a later stage a Parliamentary Board and the G 10 Commission would eventually oversight the whole process.

[81] Klass at [55].

[82] The reactive and minimalist approach taken by the UK legislator has, however, been heavily criticized. See e.g. B. Goold, Liberty and others v The United Kingdom: a new chance for another missed opportunity, 2009 Public Law 5.

[83] (2011) 52 E.H.R.R. 4 (Kennedy).

[84] Kennedy at [128].

[85] Kennedy at [159].

rity"[86] and "serious crimes"[87]) and that the categories of persons liable to have their communications intercepted was also clear for interception of communications could only be a measure of targeted surveillance,[88] as well as the provisions on duration, renewal and cancellation of interception warrants.[89] Substantial safeguards were also in place such as administrative (by the Interception of Communications Commissioner) and judicial oversight (by the Investigatory Powers Tribunal). This said, despite the allegation by the applicant that the interception was not needed to safeguard national security,[90] the Court was not really able to assess the conformity and proportionality of the actual interception activity having allegedly taken place.[91] The Court simply assessed the quality of the legal framework.

The advent of the Internet and growth of new technologies saw the development of techniques of "strategic monitoring" or mass surveillance. In recent years, the ECtHR had thus to assess twice the legality of interceptions of communications run on a large scale to gather intelligence that might allow preventive action. While the ECtHR condemned the UK practice in Liberty v UK,[92] it could be argued that the ECtHR remains too deferential to state interests. This seems to be clear in particular if one dives into the first case Weber and Saravia v Germany.[93] However, there should be enough in these cases to condemn recent practices such as the Tempora programme.[94]

In Weber, the first applicant was a freelance journalist who worked for various German and foreign media and in particular investigated matters of interest for the Federal Intelligence Service, ranging from drug and arm trafficking to preparations for war and including money laundering. To pursue her investigation, she was often operating abroad. She complained in particular about certain provisions of the Act of August 13, 1968, on Restrictions on the Secrecy of Mail, Post and Telecommunications, (the G10 Act) which allowed the strategic monitoring of any individual. In other words, the G10 Act authorised the monitoring of international wireless telecommunications in order to identify and avoid certain dangers such as an armed attack on the Federal Republic of Germany, the commission of international terrorist attacks in the Federal Republic of Germany, international arms

---

[86] The ECtHR relies upon a definition to be found in a 1986 Report: "[A]ctivities which threaten the safety of well-being of the State, and which are intended to undermine or overthrow Parliamentary democracy by political, industrial or violent means". See Kennedy at [33].

[87] See Sect. 81 of RIPA 2000.

[88] Kennedy at [160]. See Sect. 8(1) which provides that "an interception warrant must name or describe either—(a) one person as the interception subject; or (b) a single set of premises as the premises in relation to which the interception to which the warrant relates is to take place".

[89] Kennedy at [161].

[90] Kennedy at [14].

[91] Kenney at [155].

[92] (2009) 48 E.H.R.R. 1 at [69–70] (Liberty).

[93] (2008) 46 E.H.R.R. SE5.

[94] see infra pp. 54-55

trafficking, prohibited external trade in goods, data-processing programmes and technologies in cases of considerable importance, illegal importation of drugs in substantial quantities into the territory of the Federal Republic of Germany.

Unsurprisingly, the Court in Weber starts by recalling the upshots of its precedent case law: "In its case law on secret measures of surveillance, the Court has developed the following minimum safeguards that should be set out in statute law in order to avoid abuses of power: the nature of the offences which may give rise to an interception order; a definition of the categories of people liable to have their telephones tapped; a limit on the duration of telephone tapping; the procedure to be followed for examining, using and storing the data obtained; the precautions to be taken when communicating the data to other parties; and the circumstances in which recordings may or must be erased or the tapes destroyed".[95]

Nevertheless, applying these principles to the facts of the case it held that strategic monitoring under the G10 Act "was embedded into a legislative context providing considerable safeguards against abuse" and was therefore justifiable on the ground of Article 8(2). Of particular importance were the facts that the selection of the communications to be listened to or read was made only on the basis of generic catchwords,[96] that the use of personal data relating to these communications was limited to a closed list of purposes, that upon destruction of these data the data subjects had to be notified, and that the monitoring measures were reviewed by two independent bodies. The fact that the categories of people liable to have their communications intercepted were not precisely defined was thus ignored. The Court did note though that personal data obtained through the means of personal monitoring could only be used if the person concerned was either subject to measures of targeted surveillance ("individual monitoring") or if "there were factual indications for suspecting a person of planning, committing or having committed one of the offences" in s.2 of the Act (Weber at [33]). Furthermore, it observed that the Federal Constitution Court had required that these personal data be marked and bound up with the purposes which had justified their collection.[97]

In Liberty, where practices of mass interception of communications coming from Dublin to London and on to the continent between 1990 and 1997 were at stake,[98] because all the safeguards identified by the ECtRH in Weber were missing, the Court did not need to concentrate its attention upon the categories of people liable to have their communications intercepted. As a result, the "filtering process", consisting in intercepting communications between the United Kingdom and an external source, under a warrant pursuant to s.8(4) of RIPA 2000 amounted to an unjustifiable interference to the right to respect for private life.

---

[95] Weber at [95].

[96] It was not possible to use catchwords containing features allowing the interception of specific telecommunications and thereby expressly monitor specific individuals. Weber at [32].

[97] Weber at [33–35].

[98] The applicants were claiming that between 1990 and 1997 "all public telecommunications, including telephone, facsimile and email communications, carried on microwave radio between the two British Telecom's radio stations (at Clwyd and Chester), a link which also carried much of Ireland's telecommunications traffic" had been intercepted. Liberty at [5].

All in all, despite the limits of the recent ECtHR's case law, it should be clear that even in cases in which national security interests are alleged to be at stake, Article 8 is applicable and the Court does scrutinise the appropriateness of the surveillance measure by determining whether the legal basis for the measure is accessible and foreseeable and whether the measure is proportionate to the aim pursued.

Monitoring of Communications

The Malone case is noteworthy for it involved two types of disruptive practices: the interception of correspondence strictly speaking and the technique of metering. The technique known as "metering" is said by the Court to "involve the use of a device (a metre check printer) which registers the numbers dialled on a particular telephone and the time and duration of each call". As a result, "[i]n making such records, the Post Office—now British Telecommunications—[made] use only of signals sent to itself as the provider of the telephone service and [did] not monitor or intercept telephone conversations at all".[99] From this, the UK Government had drawn the conclusion that such a technique could not amount to a violation of Article 8.[100] The answer of the ECtHR is, however, clear: "[t]he Court does not accept … that the use of data obtained from metering, whatever the circumstances and purposes, cannot give rise to an issue under Article 8".[101] In fact, there is a prima facie breach of Article 8(1) when such a technique is used to the benefit of the police. Indeed, "[t]he records of metering contain information, in particular the numbers dialled, which is an integral element in the communications made by telephone".[102] This thus means that both the content of communication and the identity of the recipient are protected by the right to the respect of one's private life, even though telecommunications providers monitor the time and duration of each call by collecting and storing numbers dialled by their customers.

The Malone judgment remains slightly ambiguous though. The ECtHR felt the need to add a rider: that of the consent of the subscriber. To use its words "release of that information [metering information] to the police without the consent of the subscriber also amounts, in the opinion of the Court, to an interference with a right guaranteed by Article 8".[103] The questions that remain open after Malone are therefore whether consent given at the time of the subscription (and not after the communication has taken place) would suffice to put such a technique outside the domain of Article 8 in all cases and whether consent plays a similar role for interception of communication as such. The Malone case was an easy case, a case decided before the boom of privacy policies. Consent was not characterised. In the end, the ECtHR was thus able to state that because there were no legal rules

---

[99] Malone at [83].

[100] Malone at [83].

[101] Malone at [84].

[102] Malone at [84].

[103] Malone at [84].

concerning the scope and manner of exercise of the discretion enjoyed by the public authorities to require information relating to the time, duration and recipient of telephone calls, such a technique could not be ordered in "accordance with the law" and thereby failed to comply with Article 8(2) requirements.[104]

The collection and storage of data, and in particular data pertaining to communications, have been significantly eased with the diffusion of the Internet. It is thus logically that the ECtHR held in Copland v United Kingdom[105] that the collection and storage of information derived from the monitoring of emails as well as "information derived from the monitoring of personal Internet usage"[106] amounted to a breach of Article 8(1). In this case, the applicant was claiming that its employer (a public body for whose actions the State was directly responsible under the ECHR) had breached Article 8 by monitoring its emails and Internet usages. By monitoring of emails, one must understand the analysis of email addresses and dates and times at which emails were sent,[107] and by monitoring of personal Internet usage, the analysis of the websites visited, the times and dates of the visits to the websites and their duration.[108]

The ECtHR expressly confirmed that for the purposes of Article 8 "[t]he mere fact that these data may have been legitimately obtained by the [employer], in the form of telephone bills, [was] no bar to finding an interference with rights guaranteed under Art. 8".[109] The fact that some have legitimate access to the personal information at stake is thus irrelevant as much as the fact that the personal information collected and stored was not ultimately disclosed or used against the applicant in disciplinary or other proceedings.[110] In the case at hand because "there was no domestic law regulating monitoring at the relevant time", the interference was not, "in accordance with the law".[111]

Truly, the ECtHR did not give much explanation as regards why it is that the monitoring of communication falls within Article 8(1). Said otherwise, it did not explain what the danger of allowing the systematic surveillance of online behaviour was. But the court clearly stated that the content of communications and the numbers dialled allowing an identification of the recipient of the communications were intimately linked, the former being in reality an "integral element of the communications made by telephone"[112] as already mentioned in Malone.[113] This makes sense given the bi-dimension of the right to the protection of one's private

---

[104] Malone at [87].

[105] (2007) 45 E.H.R.R. 37 (Copland).

[106] Copland at [41].

[107] Copland at [13].

[108] Copland at [11].

[109] Copland at [43].

[110] Copland at [43].

[111] Copland at [49]. The Regulation of Investigatory Powers Act 2000 and thereby the Telecommunications (Lawful Business Practice) Regulations 2000 came into force after the facts on the case.

[112] Copland at [43].

[113] Malone at [84].

life which comprises of both the right to respect of secrecy of private life and the right to respect of liberty of private life in order to fully secure individuals' personal autonomy and human dignity. However, in the end, it is not clear whether the distinction between interception of communication and monitoring of communication is really appropriate as the debate surrounding the distinction between content data and traffic data shows it.[114]

This said, the ECtHR noted that "since the conduct alleged consisted of monitoring and not interception, the nature of such interference was of a significantly lower order of seriousness than the cases mentioned above".[115] Although this observation does seem to be relevant mainly for the sake of calculating the appropriate amount of damages due, it transpires from the formulation used by the ECtHR that it did opine that monitoring of information is less serious than interception of communication as such.

What remained unclear after Copland is the scope of the rider inserted by the ECtHR. The ECtHR observed that "[t]he applicant in the present case had been given no warning that her calls would be liable to monitoring, therefore she had a reasonable expectation as to the privacy of calls made from her work telephone. The same expectation should apply in relation to the applicant's email and internet usage".[116] Such a qualification would mean, a contrario, that if the employer had given the employee prior warning that her call would be liable to monitoring no breach of Article 8(1) could have been characterised in the first place. The foregoing would hold true irrespective of the aim pursued by the employer. While such a result could perhaps be justified in the workplace, which has traditionally been less protected than the home,[117] it is arguable whether warnings (which are not tantamount to consent at least in theory) should always suffice to transform an interference into a lawful activity, and ultimately, whether the reasoning used by the ECtHR should be applied by analogy in the context of user-to-information society providers relationships given the opacity of privacy policies.[118] Because Copland was primarily about monitoring of communication one could argue though that the rider would only be relevant in cases of monitoring and note cases of interceptions.

Hopefully a few years later, the ECtHR clarified its reasoning by stating in particular in Köpke v Germany that "[a] person's reasonable expectations as to privacy is a significant though not necessarily conclusive factor".[119] It remains to be seen though in which cases warnings and eventually consent will be decisive.

---

[114] See infra pp.

[115] Copland at [54].

[116] Copland at [42].

[117] See e.g. Niemietz.

[118] In most cases, users are not in practice able to freely express a choice in relation to the terms of online service providers' privacy policies.

[119] Köpke v Germany (2011) 53 E.H.R.R. SE26 at [37]. See also ECtHR Gillan and Quinton v United Kingdom Judgment 12 January 2010, at [61]; PG v United Kingdom (2008) 46 E.H.R.R. 51 (PG) at [57]; Perry v United Kingdom (2004) 39 E.H.R.R. 3 at [37]. But see Halford v United Kingdom (1997) 24 E.H.R.R. 523 at [45].

Collection and Storage of Information Relating to Physical Identity

Telephone wiretapping not only implies the interception of communication, thereby content data, but it also allows the recording of the voice of the persons communicating together, a piece of information pertaining to physical identity.

While most of the cases dealing with telephone wiretapping, or other more intrusive methods of investigation, implied the storage of information relating to physical identity, the principle of the secrecy of the correspondence or of the premise at stake (the home or the businesses premises) was enough to justify the characterisation of a violation of Article 8(1).

The ECtHR has, however, extended its definition of private life to include information relating to physical identity, even in cases where the information has not been collected through the means of an interception or from within secluded places. This has been the case in particular when sensitive data have been collected and subsequently stored, such as genetic information, or when the visual or oral image of a person has been recorded.

In S and Marper v United Kingdom,[120] the first applicant, Mr S, had been arrested at the age of 11 and charged with attempted robbery. His fingerprints and DNA samples were taken but he was subsequently acquitted. The second applicant, Mr Marper, had been arrested and charged with harassment of his partner. His fingerprints and DNA samples were taken. However, before a pretrial review took place, the charges had been dropped. Both applicants asked for their fingerprints and DNA samples to be destroyed, but in both cases, the police and the national courts refused. The applicants thus complained under Art. 8 of the ECHR about the retention of their fingerprints, cellular samples and DNA profiles. The ECtHR held that as a matter of principle "[t]he mere storing of data relating to the private life of an individual amounts to an interference within the meaning of art. 8. The subsequent use of the stored information has no bearing on that finding. However, in determining whether the personal information retained by the authorities involves any of the private-life aspects mentioned above, the Court will have due regard to the specific context in which the information at issue has been recorded and retained, the nature of the records, the way in which these records are used and processed and the results that may be obtained".[121]

Applying these principles to the facts at hand, the ECtHR noted that fingerprints, cellular samples and DNA profiles were personal data within the meaning of the Data Protection Convention.[122] Despite the impossibility to characterise any misuse of these personal data, the ECtHR found that their retention amounted to

---

[120]   (2009) 48 E.H.R.R. 50 (S and Marper).

[121]   S and Marper, at [67].

[122]   (ETS No. 108). The Convention for the Protection of Individuals with regard to Automatic Processing of Personal Data was drawn up within the Council of Europe by a committee of governmental experts under the authority of the European Committee on Legal Co-operation (CDCJ) and was opened for signature by the member States of the Council of Europe on 28 January 1981 in Strasbourg.

an interference with the right to respect for private life. Indeed, future misuses adversely affecting the private-life interests of the applicants could not be fore-closed.[123] In addition, cellular samples contained sensitive data and a substantial amount of unique personal data that "went well beyond neutral identification".[124]

As regards the application of Article 8(2), the ECtHR first noted that "[t]he inter-ests of the data subjects and the community as a whole in protecting the personal data, including fingerprint and DNA information, may be outweighed by the legitimate interest in the prevention of crime. However, the intrinsically private character of this information call[ed] for the Court to exercise careful scrutiny of any state measure authorising its retention and use by the authorities without the consent of the person concerned".[125] The analysis of the ECtHR focused upon the proportionality of the measure. Remarkably, the ECtHR attempted to assess the degree of effectiveness of the retention measure in relation to its aim[126] to finally opine that the extension of the DNA database had contributed to the detection and prevention of crime.[127] However, the interference could not be justified given the "the blanket and indiscriminate nature of the power of retention".[128] In this sense, the S and Marper case was an easy case.

As regards images of individuals, the ECtHR has followed the same lines, although voices and pictures are certainly less sensitive than genetic information. Generally speaking, the ECtHR has recognised that "a person's image constitutes one of the chief attributes of his or her personality, as it reveals the person's unique characteristics and distinguishes the person from his or her peers. The right to the protection of one's image is thus one of the essential components of personal development. It mainly presupposes the individual's right to control the use of that image, including the right to refuse publication thereof".[129]

In PG v United Kingdom,[130] concerning among other things the use of listening devices in the police station, the ECtHR considered that a permanent record of a

---

[123] S and Marper, at [71].

[124] S and Marper, at [72].

[125] S and Marper, at [104].

[126] S and Marper, at [116–117].

[127] S and Marper, at [117].

[128] S and Marper, at [119]: "The material may be retained irrespective of the nature or gravity of the offence with which the individual was originally suspected or of the age of the suspected offender; fingerprints and samples may be taken—and retained—from a person of any age, arrested in connection with a recordable offence, which includes minor or non-imprisonable offences. The retention is not time limited; the material is retained indefinitely whatever the nature or seriousness of the offence of which the person was suspected. Moreover, there exist only limited possibilities for an acquitted individual to have the data removed from the nationwide database or the materi-als destroyed; in particular, there is no provision for independent review of the justification for the retention according to defined criteria, including such factors as the seriousness of the offence, pre-vious arrests, the strength of the suspicion against the person and any other special circumstances". Besides, the interests of minors were not specifically taken into account.

[129] Von Hannover v Germany S [2012] E.M.L.R. 16 at [96]. See also Reklos v Greece [2009] E.M.L.R. 16 at [40].

[130] PG v United Kingdom (2008) 46 E.H.R.R. 51 (PG).

person's voice for further analysis was of direct relevance to identifying that person when considered in conjunction with other personal data.[131] It did thus amount to an interference with the applicant's right to respect for private life. The ECtHR stated clearly that "[t]here are a number of elements relevant to a consideration of whether a person's private life is concerned by measures effected outside a person's home or private premises. Since there are occasions when people knowingly or intentionally involve themselves in activities which are or may be recorded or reported in a public manner, a person's reasonable expectations as to privacy may be a significant, although not necessarily conclusive, factor. A person who walks down the street will, inevitably, be visible to any member of the public who is also present. Monitoring by technological means of the same public scene (for example, a security guard viewing through closed-circuit television) is of a similar character. Private-life considerations may arise, however, once any systematic or permanent record comes into existence of such material from the public domain".[132] The systematic or permanent recording of personal information relating to physical identity (including personal information to be found in the public domain) thus transforms it into private information. As a result, mass surveillance practices implying the collection and storage of publicly available personal information relating to physical identity amounts to a prima facie interference with the right to respect for private life.

A fortiori, when the systematic collection and storage of individuals' images is followed by misuse, such as the diffusion of the image to members of the public, it is hard not to characterise a violation of the right to respect for private life. In Peck[133], the applicant complained that the disclosure by the Brentwood Borough council of a CCTV footage, which resulted in the publication and broadcasting of identifiable images of him,[134] constituted a disproportionate interference with his

---

[131] PG at [59–60]. Therefore, the interference was not "in accordance with the law" as required by para. 2 of Art. 8. PG at [63]. Compare with Friedl (1996) 21 E.H.R.R. 83 at [49–51] in which the Commission considered that the retention of anonymous photographs that had been taken at a public demonstration did not interfere with the right to respect for private life. In so deciding, it attached special weight to the fact that the photographs concerned had not been entered in a data-processing system and that the authorities had taken no steps to identify the persons photographed by means of data processing. In a more recent case the mere collection of personal information was prohibited. Reklos v Greece [2009] E.M.L.R. 16. The applicant was a child though.

[132] PG at [57].

[133] Peck v United Kingdom [2003] E.M.L.R. 15 (Peck). See also Perry v United Kingdom (2004) 39 E.H.R.R. 3 (Perry) at [40–43] in which the ECtHR found that because the footage of the applicant had been taken for use in a video identification procedure and, potentially, as evidence prejudicial to his defence at trial the recording and the use of the footage amounted to a violation of Article 8(1). Besides it was not possible to justify the violation on the ground of Article 8(2) for it was not done "in accordance with the law". Perry at [49].

[134] At night, the applicant had been walking towards a central junction in the centre of Brentwood with a kitchen knife in his hand and attempted suicide by cutting his wrists. He had stopped at the junction and leaned over a railing facing the traffic with the knife in his hand. He had not been unaware that a CCTV camera, mounted on the traffic island in front of the junction, filmed his movements. The CCTV footage later disclosed did show the applicant in possession of a knife. The cutting of the wrists was not part of the footage.

right to respect for his private life guaranteed by Art. 8. The ECtHR ruled that although the disclosure pursued the legitimate aim of public safety, the prevention of disorder and crime and the protection of the rights of others, the disclosure did have a basis in law and was, with appropriate legal advice, foreseeable, it was not necessary in a democratic society.[135] The ECtHR noted that this case did not involve the disclosure of footage of the commission of a crime.[136] Importantly, it added that other less intrusive options had been available to the council for it to achieve the same objectives.[137] The ECtHR thus concluded that "in the circumstances of this case, there were [not] relevant or sufficient reasons which would justify the direct disclosure by the council to the public of stills from the footage in own publication CCTV News without the council obtaining the applicant's consent or masking his identity, or which would justify its disclosures to the media without the council taking steps to ensure so far as possible that such masking would be effected by the media. The crime prevention objective and context of the disclosures demanded particular scrutiny and care in these respects in the present case".[138]

Other cases could also be cited. In Von Hannover, the ECtHR held that the publication of photographs of the applicant[139] in her daily life, alone, or with other persons, fell within the scope of her private life and could not be justified on the ground of a public interest because it did not aim at "contributing to a debate of general interest".[140]

In Köpke, the applicant had been employed as a shop assistant and cashier in a supermarket. Her employer suspected the applicant and another employee of having manipulated the accounts. With the help of a detective agency, the employer carried out covert video surveillance of the supermarket's drinks department. The camera covered the area behind the cash desk including the till, the cashier and the area immediately surrounding the cash desk. After having received the report of the detective agency, the applicant's employer dismissed the applicant without notice for theft. The applicant contested the validity of her dismissal and objected to the use of the covert video surveillance, arguing that this surveillance had breached her right to protection of her privacy, before national courts and then before the ECtHR.

Köpke, although an admissibility decision, is interesting for at least three reasons. Firstly, it confirms that the concept of private life is intertwined with the notion of personal identity and therefore extends beyond the interception or monitoring of communications. "The Court reiterate[ed] that the concept of private life

---

[135] Peck at [67].

[136] Peck at [79].

[137] Peck at [80–84].

[138] Peck at [85].

[139] A public figure.

[140] Von Hannover v Germany [2004] E.M.L.R. 21. Notably although only the publication of the photos seemed to be at stake, the applicant had alleged that "as soon as she left her house she was constantly hounded by paparazzi who followed her every daily movement, be it crossing the road, fetching her children from school, doing her shopping, out walking, practising sport or going on holiday". Von Hannover at [44].

extends to aspects relating to personal identity, such as a person's name or pic-ture".[141] Furthermore, in the case at hand it was deemed that the recording of a person's conduct amounted to "a considerable intrusion into the employee's pri-vate life. It entails a recorded and reproducible documentation of a person's con-duct at his or her workplace, which the employee, being obliged under the employment contract to perform the work in that place, [could not] evade".[142]

Secondly, it reaffirms that the balancing to be undertaken in cases in which posi-tive obligations are imposed upon public authority to make sure Article 8 is com-plied with in the framework of private parties' relationships is very close to the test of Article 8(2). Indeed, the ECtHR stated that "in certain circumstances, the state's positive obligation under Art. 8 is only adequately complied with if the state safe-guards respect for private life in the relations of individuals between themselves by legislative provisions providing a framework for reconciling the various interests that compete for protection in the relevant context".[143] The ECtHR thus looked for the existence of a legal basis to be assessed under the traditional 3-prong test.

Thirdly, when considering whether the public authority involved had struck a fair balance between the applicant's right to respect for her private life, her employer's interest in protection of his property rights,[144] and the public interest in the proper administration of justice, the ECtHR noted that one important safeguard was present: the fact that prior to the implementation of the surveillance measure there existed suspicions as regards the behaviour of the applicant: she was sus-pected by her employer of having committed a criminal offence.[145] It was thus a measure of targeted surveillance and not a measure of mass surveillance. Besides, although the ECtHR has been helped by the national court, it observed that "the domestic courts considered that there had not been any other equally effective means to protect the employer's property rights which would have interfered to a lesser extent with the applicant's right to respect for her private life".[146] The ECtHR was thus able to conclude that the application had to be dismissed[147] after having scrutinised the proportionality of the surveillance measure at stake.

Going back to national law and in particular English law, it should now be clear why the retention of the photographs by the police in the Regina (Wood) v Commissioner of Police of the Metropolis[148] case was held to be unlawful by the Court of Appeal despite the strength of the dissenting opinion. In this case, a police officer had taken and retained the photographs of the claimant walking in the streets of London while leaving Reed Elsevier plc's annual general meeting to

---

[141] Köpke at [36].

[142] Köpke at [46].

[143] Köpke at [42].

[144] Guaranteed by art. 1 of Protocol No. 1 to the Convention.

[145] Köpke at [44].

[146] Köpke at [50].

[147] Köpke at [53].

[148] [2009] EWCA Civ 414 (Wood).

which he had gone to find some information about Reed's indirect involvement in
the arms trade. The reason for his being photographed was that he had been seen
in the company of an activist who "had a history of violent protests and who, it
was believed, had a tendency to encourage otherwise peaceful protesters to commit offences".[149]Although one could argue that Article 8(1) should only be
engaged when the interference is serious enough[150] and the mere taking of someone's photograph in a public street should not be considered as amounting to
breach of any right unless something more is added,[151] when the images are
retained for surveillance purposes the measure should always be scrutinised in particular when the process is automated. As a result, in this case, the measure was
neither in "accordance with the law" nor proportionate. Lord Collins of
Mapessbury rightly noted that the taking of the photographs was "lawful at common law, and that there [was] nothing to prevent their retention".[152] But while
"there [was] a published policy by the Metropolitan Police on the use of overt
filming and photography",[153] there was nothing on the retention of photographs.
The national law, broadly defined, did not specify the duration of the retention, nor
the reason for the retention or the mechanism for oversight. It was not clear which
types of crimes would trigger retention and which categories of individuals could
be concerned.[154] In addition, "the retention of the photographs for more than a few
days could not be justified as furthering the aim of detecting the perpetrators of
any crime that may have been committed during the meeting".[155] The threat at
issue was not that of terrorism but that of a low-level crime and disorder.[156]

---

[149] Wood at [69].

[150] Wood at [22] as per Laws LJ dissenting in this case. This approach is, however, dangerous
in so far as it amounts to lowering the requirement for legality when the interference appears
to be modest. Indeed, if modest inferences are repeated, it is, however, possible to create a very
detailed profile of the individuals monitored. See Wood at [54]. In addition, it can lead to the formulation of an oversimplified test like the test used by Lord Hope of Craighead DPSC in Kinloch
v HM Advocate [2012] UKSC 62. The answer is to be found not only by considering whether the
alleged victim had a reasonable expectation of privacy while she was in public view but also by
considering whether the interference was a measure of surveillance and whether the information
had subsequently been stored through the means in particular of an automated process.

[151] Wood at [35] as per Laws LJ dissenting.

[152] Wood at [98].

[153] Wood at [98].

[154] The only relevant information found was the following: "The Metropolitan Police Service
('MPS') is committed to providing MPS personnel with a particularly useful tactic to combat
crime and gather intelligence and evidence relating to street crime, anti-social behaviour and
public order. It may be used to record identifiable details of subjects suspected of being involved
in crime or anti-sociable [sic] behaviour such as facial features, visible distinctive marks e g, tat-
toos, jewellery, clothing and associates for the purposes of preventing and detecting crime and to
assist in the investigation for all alleged offences. This tactic may also be used to record officers'
actions in the following circumstances" Wood at [13].

[155] Wood at [97].

[156] Wood at [84] per Dyson LJ.

Collection and Storage of Publicly Accessible Information

Surveillance does not necessarily imply the interception or the monitoring of communications. It can also consist in gathering all types of information about individuals that are publicly accessible including but not limited to the taking of photographs in public places. What matters is the systematic character or the permanence of the record. For this reason, it is without difficulties that the ECtHR held quite early in the Leander case[157] that prima facie both the storing and the release of information about one's private life, as well as the refusal to allow the subject an opportunity to refute the information, amounted to an interference with the right to respect for private life secured by Article 8(1).[158]

The Leander case had been brought by a Swedish citizen who was a carpenter by profession. On 20 August 1979, the applicant had started to work as a temporary replacement in the post of museum technician which was vacant for 10 months at the Naval Museum at Karlskrona in the south of Sweden. Yet, the museum was adjacent to the Karlskrona Naval Base which was a restricted military security zone. After a month, the applicant was told that the outcome of the personnel control undertaken in pursuance of the Personnel Control Ordinance 1969 had been unfavourable and that he could not be employed at the Museum anymore.[159] Following the advice of the Security Chief of the Naval Base, the applicant wrote to the Commander-in-Chief of the Navy, requesting to be informed of the reasons why he could not be employed at the Naval Museum, and the latter answered that his assessment from a security point of view had ended being negative so that a decision had been taken not to accept him. The applicant complained to the government which requested the opinion of the Supreme Commander of the Armed Forces, who in turn consulted the Commander-in-Chief of the Navy. The Commander-in-chief explained that the person employed in the post in question had to have free access to, and freedom to circulate in, the Naval Base. This would have meant that the person employed would have had access to secret installations and information. Therefore, given the results of the personal control of the applicant, the latter could not be offered the job. To be more precise the ultimate opinion of the Supreme Commander of the Armed Forces was followed by a secret annex, containing a report on Mr. Leander released by the National Police Board. Yet, this annex had never been communicated to the applicant.[160] The applicant subsequently complained to the government. The government like the National Policy Board refused to give the applicant access to the secret police information at stake. The applicant before the ECtHR therefore claimed among other things that the personal control procedure as applied in this case amounted to a breach of Article 8.

---

[157] Leander v Sweden (1987) 9 E.H.R.R. 433 (Leander).

[158] Leander at [48].

[159] It seems, at least according to the Swedish government, that two mistakes had been made by the Director of the Museum: First he took the decision to employ the applicant before the communication of the results of the personal control and second the post had not properly been declared vacant. Leander at [10].

[160] Besides, it was not included in the material submitted to the Court. Leander at [14].

The Leander case, decided in 1987, showed quite early the limit of the explicatory value of the paradigm of secrecy and the intimate connection between the concept of private life and that of personal autonomy and human dignity, although the ECtHR did not expressly use these terms. Indeed in this case, the Swedish police had gathered information about the applicant as regards his past activities and stored it in a secret police register. Notably, the rule in force was that in this register no entry could be inserted for the reason that a person, by belonging to an organisation or by other means, had expressed a political opinion.[161] The arguments put forward by the applicant implied, though, that it was arguable that such a prohibition had not been complied with.[162] Still, on the basis of this information, the Director of the Museum had taken the decision not to employ the applicant. The notion of private life in this case thus encompassed both private and public aspects of the applicant's life. Said otherwise, in this case, the concern was not the fact that a secluded sphere had been intruded by unwanted eyes but the fact that some had routinely and systematically collected a wide range of information including publicly accessible information about an individual to possibly exert some degree of power over that individual. Personal autonomy, more than secrecy, was at stake there.

That being said, although in this case there was a breach of Article 8(1), the ECtHR ultimately found the procedure justified on the ground of Article 8(2). First of all the aim of the Swedish personnel control system, including the creation and maintenance of the secret police register, was legitimate under Article 8 for it was alleged to serve the protection of national security.[163] Notably, the ECtHR did not attempt to give a definition of the term of national security for national governments and law-enforcement bodies have a wide discretion in this field. Second, the interference at stake had a legal basis in domestic law. Third, this legal basis was accessible. Fourth, it was foreseeable. The ECtRH recalled that in the field of national security, the requirement of foreseeability must be given a specific meaning: "it cannot mean that an individual should be enabled to foresee precisely what checks will be made in his regard by the Swedish special police service in its efforts to protect national security". But referring to the Malone case the ECtHR added that "the law has to be sufficiently clear in its terms to give [individuals] an

---

[161] Leander at [19].

[162] The ECtHR observed that "[r]egarding his personal background, [the applicant] furnished the following details to the Commission and the Court. At the relevant time, he had not belonged to any political party since 1976. Earlier he had been a member of the Swedish Communist Party. He had also been a member of an association publishing a radical review—Fib/Kulturfront. During his military service, in 1971–1972, he had been active in the soldiers' union and a representative at the soldiers' union conference in 1972 which, according to him, had been infiltrated by the security police. His only criminal conviction stems from his time in military service and consisted of a fine of 10 Skr. for having been late for a military parade. He had also been active in the Swedish Building Workers' Association and he had travelled a couple of times in Eastern Europe. The applicant asserted however that, according to unanimous statements by responsible officials, none of the abovementioned circumstances should have been the cause for the unfavourable outcome of the personnel control". Leander at [17].

[163] Leander at [48].

adequate indication as to the circumstances in which and the conditions on which the public authorities are empowered to resort to this kind of secret and potentially dangerous interference with private life".[164] In any case, despite the existence of administrative instructions or practices "the law itself must clearly indicate the scope of the discretion conferred on the competent authority with sufficient clarity, having regard to the legitimate aim of the measure in question, to give the individual adequate protection against arbitrary interference".[165] Applying these principles in the case at hand the ECtHR held that Swedish law laid down, with sufficient precision, the conditions under which the National Police Board were empowered to store and release information under the personnel control system.[166] The interference at issue was therefore in "accordance with the law".[167] Fifth, that same interference was also found to be "necessary in a democratic society".

At this final stage, the ECtHR had to balance two competing interests: that of the applicant for the respect of his private life and that of the government for the protection of national security. More precisely, the ECtHR had to check whether Swedish law contained enough appropriate safeguards to make the personnel control system meet the requirements of Article 8(2).[168] The ECtHR thus attempted to undertake a control of proportionality of the interference in relation to the aim pursued by the measure.[169] In other words, and this is crucial, the implication of national security interests did not mean that the interference at stake could not be scrutinised. In fact, what the ECtHR did was just that, as it had paved the way in Klass. Nevertheless, it is true to say that in the field of national security, the ECtHR remains very deferential to national public authorities. In this regard, it is interesting to note that in this case, just like in Klass, the interference was justified. What seems to have been of prevalent importance was the existence of a control entrusted to independent institutions. Parliamentarians sat on the National Police Board. The Chancellor of Justice, the Parliamentary Ombudsman as well as the Parliamentary Committee on Justice, exerted an oversight of the whole process. As a result, it was possible to hold that because access to the secret police registry would compromise the efficacy of that very measure such a safeguard was not a sine qua non condition to guarantee the proportionality of the measure.

The Leander's judgment remains more problematic than the Klass one though. In Leander, the ECtHR acknowledged that the information stored could be used for

---

[164] Leander at [51].

[165] Leander at [51].

[166] Leander at [55]: "[T]he Ordinance contains explicit and detailed provisions as to what information may be handed out, the authorities to which information may be communicated, the circumstances in which such communication may take place and the procedure to be followed by the National Police Board when taking decisions to release information".

[167] Leander at [57].

[168] Leander at [67].

[169] Leander at [67]. The ECtHR expressly stated that "[t]he interference to which Mr. Leander was subjected [could not] therefore be said to have been disproportionate to the legitimate aim pursued". Leander at [67].

other purposes and in particular cases of public prosecution and cases concerning the obtaining of Swedish citizenship.[170] This is where it appears that although more discretion should be afforded to public authorities when national security interests are at stake, the line between national security and the prevention and detection of crimes in general is in fact unstable and above all not always drawn. With this said, what should be recalled from Leander is the persistence of a scrutiny in national security cases even if the scrutiny was in this case too deferential to state interests.[171]

Segerstedt Wiberg v Sweden decided in 2006[172] confirmed the willingness of the ECtHR to go further in its control of national security measures.[173] This case echoes Leander. It involved once again applicants attempting to challenge refusals to grant them full access to their Security Police records justified by the consideration that full disclosure could not be allowed without jeopardising the purpose of the measures taken or anticipated or without harming future operations. Since the Leander judgment, the legal basis had been modified. Prior to April 1, 1999,[174] absolute secrecy was the principal rule as regards access to information kept by the Security Police. The absolute secrecy rules had been abolished by an amendment to the Secrecy Act, made at the same time as the Police Data Act entered into force on April 1, 1999. While the principle remained that the information to be found in the Security Police's files was to remain secret, if it was evident that the information could be revealed without detriment to the aim of measures that had already been decided upon or that were anticipated, or without harm to future activities, the information should now be disclosed. However, the applicants maintained that the legal basis was not formulated with sufficient precision to enable them to foresee—even with the assistance of legal advice—the consequences of their own conduct and whether or not an entry could be made under their name in the Security Police files. Indeed, the Security Police's register could contain personal information about persons suspected of having engaged in or of intending to engage in criminal activity that entailed a threat to national security or a terrorist

---

[170] Leander at [64].

[171] By looking at the way the ECtHR applied Article 8(2) in both Leander (decided in 1987) and Kruslin (decided in 1990), it could appear that the framework used by the ECtHR to assess the legitimacy of the interference at stake has evolved and has become more stringent over time. While in Leander the ECtHR did not take into account the existing safeguards to assess the quality of the legal basis but examined them to determine whether the interference was proportionate to the aim pursued, in Kruslin, the safeguards were mentioned and analysed at an earlier stage, to determine whether the legal basis was foreseeable. Therefore, in Kruslin, the ECtHR did not need to address the issue of proportionality.

[172] (2007) 44 E.H.R.R. 2 (Segerstedt Wiberg).

[173] Although the safeguards to be found in national law seem to have been examined at the stage of the proportionality test more than at the stage of the quality of the legal basis test, the scrutiny does appear to be stricter.

[174] The only exceptions made were for the benefit of researchers. From 1 July 1996, it was also possible to allow exemptions if the Government held the view that there were extraordinary reasons for an exemption to be made from the main rule of absolute secrecy.

offence but also about other persons if there were other special reasons therefor.[175] The applicants were thus claiming that the foregoing rule "was excessively broad and could be applied to almost anybody".[176]

The ECtHR expressly distinguished between the storage of personal information and the refusal to give access to the record containing personal information. Both acts were considered to be breaches of Article 8(1). The Court clearly held that "the storage in the Security Police files of the information that had been released to them constituted unjustified interference with their right to respect for private life".[177] Besides, as it was implicit in the Leander case, it stated that the notion of private life should be understood broadly and comprise "even those parts of the information that were public"[178] for what really constituted the interference was the fact that "the information had been systematically collected and stored in files held by the authorities".[179]

This time, while the refusals to fully inform the applicants in relation to the data that were kept about them on the Security Police register were ultimately justified on the ground of Article 8(2), the ECtHR found that with respect to the second to fifth applicants, at least the storage of the information that had been partially released to the aforementioned applicants were not measures necessary in a democratic society. To reach that conclusion, the ECtHR observed that the continued storage of personal information could not be justified on the ground of the protection of national security because we were more than 30 years after the facts.[180] Furthermore, it seemed that the nature of the information stored, more than the currency of the events, was the paramount consideration to hold the security measure unjustifiable.[181] This is thus an important step towards increasing the intensity level of the scrutiny of national security measures.

Between the Leander and the Segerstedt Wiberg case, the ECtHR had to hear Rotaru v Romania[182] in which the applicant was requesting the amendment or destruction of files kept by the Romanian Intelligence Service. These files contained, among other things, false information as regards past political activities. While doubting that the aim pursued by such collection and storage was the protection of national security,[183] the ECtHR found the surveillance measure to be an unjustifiable

---

[175] Segerstedt-Wiberg at [49].

[176] Segerstedt-Wiberg at [74].

[177] Segerstedt-Wiberg at [70].

[178] Segerstedt-Wiberg at [72].

[179] Segerstedt-Wiberg at [72].

[180] Segerstedt-Wiberg at [90].

[181] Segerstedt-Wiberg at [91]: "In this case, the KPML(r) party programme was the only evidence relied upon by the Government. Beyond that they did not point to any specific circumstance indicating that the impugned programme clauses were reflected in actions or statements by the party's leaders or members and constituted an actual or even potential threat to national security when the information was released in 1999, almost 30 years after the party had come into existence".

[182] Rotaru v Romania (2000) 8 B.H.R.C. 449 (Rotaru).

[183] Rotaru at [53]. The ECtHR expressly stated that it had "doubts as to the relevance to national security of the information held on the applicant".

violation of Article 8 since the legal basis was not of quality.[184] Importantly in this case, the ECtHR draw a direct connection between Article 8 of the ECHR and the Council of Europe's Convention of 28 January 1981 for the Protection of Individuals with regard to Automatic Processing of Personal Data and more precisely the concept private life and that of personal data being defined in Article 2 of the Convention as "any information relating to an identified or identifiable individual".[185] This is thus logically that the ECtHR clearly stated that "public information can fall within the scope of private life where it is systematically collected and stored in files held by the authorities. That is all the truer where such information concerns a person's distant past".[186] Consequently, both the collection and storage of personal information (other than information relating to physical identity) to be found in the public domain can amount to a violation of Article 8(1). What matters is once again the systematic character of the collection and storage. Yet, surveillance relies upon the systematic collection and storage of personal information.

To sum up, although the case law of the ECtHR remains piecemeal for each decision is obviously directly tailored to the facts of the case, it does show that surveillance measures, including mass surveillance measures, are suspicious and amount to a prima facie breach of Article 8(1), even when they consist in gathering information publicly accessible. This holds true even when the ultimate purpose is the protection of national security. As a result, surveillance measures have to be scrutinised to make sure their legal bases are of quality (they are accessible and foreseeable) and the measures are necessary in a democratic society. This is illustrated by Fig. 1.2.

1.3 Privacy and Data Protection

The fundamental dichotomy between secrecy and liberty of private life is confirmed by the European Charter of Fundament Rights[187] which does not, however, exactly replicate the ECHR for it distinguishes between two human rights: the

---

[184] Rotaru at [57–62]. No provision of domestic law defined the kind of information to be recorded, the categories of people against whom surveillance measures could have taken, the circumstances in which such measures could have been taken and the procedure to be followed. The collection and storage had been limited to a certain period of time. Nothing had been said as regards the possibility to access the information contained in these files. No system of supervision of the surveillance activities had been put in place.

[185] Rotaru at [43]. See also Amann v. Switzerland [GC] ECHR 2000-II at [65].

[186] Rotaru at [43].

[187] (2000/C 364/01) OJEC C 364/1 18 December 2000. The Charter of Fundamental Rights of the European Union was signed and proclaimed in 2000 by the European Parliament, the European Commission and by the EU member states, comprising the European Council. It includes civil, political, economic and social rights and certain "third generation" rights. With the coming into force of the Treaty of Lisbon in December 2009, the Charter has been transformed into a binding instrument and is therefore directly enforceable by the Court of Justice of the European Union (CJEU) and national courts. Under Art. 6(1) of the Treaty on the European Union "the Union recognises the rights, freedoms and principles set out in the Charter of Fundamental Rights".

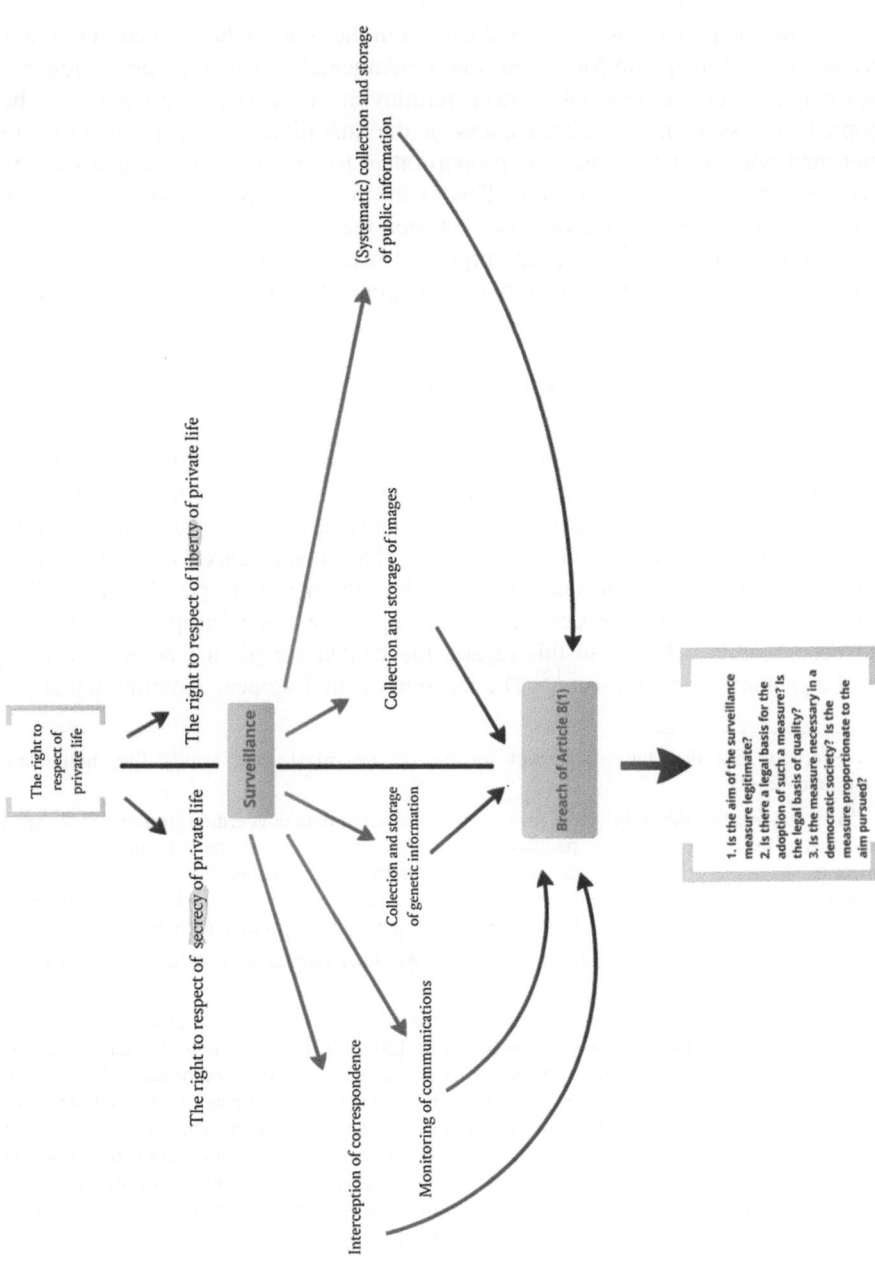

Fig. 1.2 The scrutiny of surveillance measures

right for the respect for private and family life (Art. 7)[188] and the right for the protection of personal data (Art. 8)".[189] In this sense, the European Charter is maybe less progressive than the ECHR. As it will be explained below, disconnecting[190] the right for the protection of personal data from the right to the protection of one's private life is problematic for at least one fundamental reason: data protection law does not allow one to undertake a deep scrutiny of the surveillance measure to be adopted, by assessing the effectiveness of the surveillance measure in order to determine whether the measure is proportionate to the aim pursued and thereby necessary in a democratic society. This is the reason why it is crucial to fully understand the relationship that exists between the right to respect for private life and data protection law.[191] For that purpose, it is necessary to look at both components of the European data protection regime: general principles and special rules.

1.3.1   General Data Protection Law

At this stage, it is useful to recall the early days of data protection law in Europe to fully understand the rationale that lies behind this body of rules. The laying down of a European regime for the protection of personal data was not a straightforward action for a European community which did not have competence as regards the protection of fundamental rights and liberties such as the right to respect for private life. In fact during the drafting process, the very competence of the European Community had been heavily debated. In this regard, the United Kingdom was one the most vocal disputants of the project.[192] The inaction of the European Commission at the

---

[188] "Everyone has the right to respect for his or her private and family life, home and communications".

[189] "1. Everyone has the right to the protection of personal data concerning him or her. 2. Such data must be processed fairly for specified purposes and on the basis of the consent of the person concerned or some other legitimate basis laid down by law. Everyone has the right of access to data which has been collected concerning him or her, and the right to have it rectified. 3. Compliance with these rules shall be subject to control by an independent authority".

[190] This disconnection has also been condemned by other commentators. See, e.g. Costa and Poullet [19] at 255.

[191] The similarity and complementary of traditional privacy law and data protection law are not always clearly understood. See e.g. Robinson et al. [20, p. 27]. This is how the authors of this report frame the problem: "[t]he scope of the Directive has been criticised because the relationship between privacy protection and data protection is vague: not all acts of personal data processing as covered by the Directive have a clear or noticeable privacy impact, and we must ask if this is a weakness in its focus. Should the impact on privacy be a relevant criterion for determining the applicability of data protection rules?" This is a pertinent concern only to the extent that the right to respect for private life is quite limited in scope, which does not seem to be the case.

[192] See Pearche and Platten [21] at 533. See also in France Proposition de résolution sur la proposition de directive du Conseil des Communautés européennes relative à la protection des personnes physiques à l'égard du traitement des données à caractère personnel et à la libre circulation de ces données, présentée par Robert Pandraud et Pierre Mazeaud, Assemblée nationale, 27 avril 1993, n°117.

end of the 1980s was justified by the fact that the ratification of an international convention, the Convention 108 of the Council of Europe was intended to foster harmonisation between Member States. The European Commission had encouraged Member States to sign and ratify that international text.[193] After 5 years of negotiations, the Council of Europe had adopted, on 28 January 1981, a Convention for the Protection of Individuals with regard to Automatic Processing of Personal Data which entered into force on 11 October 1985.[194] The Convention 108 tries to strike a fair balance between the protection of fundamental rights and the necessity to allow the free flow of personal data. Its scope is definitely far-reaching for it relies upon a broad definition of personal data ("'personal data' means any information relating to an identified or identifiable individual ['data subject']"[195]) and aims at regulating both the public and the private sector.[196]

Under Article 5 of the Convention, every processing of personal data has to comply with four fundamental principles: personal data shall be "obtained and processed fairly and lawfully" (principle of loyalty), personal data shall be "stored for specified and legitimate purposes and not used in a way incompatible with those purposes" and shall be "adequate, relevant and not excessive in relation to the purposes for which they are stored" (principle of finality or purpose limitation), personal data shall be "preserved in a form which permits identification of the data subjects for no longer than is required for the purpose for which those data are stored" (principle of limited duration), and the data processed shall be "accurate and, where necessary, kept up to date" (principle of accuracy). On top of these data quality principles, the Convention recognises a principle of data security in its Article 7. Several rights are granted to data subjects such as the right to information, to rectification or erasure or more generally a right to a remedy in case of non-compliance.[197]

Notably, although one of the main objectives of the Convention is to ensure "the free flow of information between peoples",[198] the protection of fundamental rights ultimately seems to prevail over the latter. Under Article 12, although parties to the Convention "shall not, for the sole purpose of the protection of privacy, prohibit or subject to special authorisation transborder flows of personal data going to the territory of another Party", they are allowed to restrict transborder flows of personal data "insofar as [their] legislation includes specific regulations for certain categories of personal data or of automated personal data files" which are more protective.

---

[193] 81/679/EEC. Commission Recommendation of 29 July 1981 relating to the Council of Europe Convention for the protection of individuals with regard to automatic processing of personal data Official Journal L 246, 29/08/1981 pp. 31–31.

[194] This Convention as of the time of writing has been ratified by 45 countries among which all the countries of the European Union. Notably this Convention is open for signature to non-members of the Council of Europe but no third-party country has taken that opportunity.

[195] Article 2.

[196] See Article 3(1): "The Parties undertake to apply this convention to automated personal data files and automatic processing of personal data in the public and private sectors".

[197] See Article 8.

[198] Preamble.

But the ratification of the Convention 108 by the Member States of the European Union was not enough to create a levelled playing field. The Convention was not self-executing and parties to the Convention had the possibility to restrain its scope of application[199] and/or go beyond the minimum standards set forth in the Convention.[200] Despite attempts to improve the framework by the adoption of recommendations (without any binding effects though) targeting specific sectors and in particular the Recommendation of 17 September 1987, regulating the use of personal data in the police sector,[201] and the adoption of the additional Protocol of the 8 November 2001[202] which tried to give an answer to the problem of data transfer to third party countries,[203] the European Commission finally took the initiative to propose the adoption of a piece of secondary legislation. Truly other instruments at the international level had been adopted in wake of the Convention 108, such as the OECD Guidelines on the Protection of Privacy and Transborder Flows of Personal Data,[204] or the UN Guidelines for the Regulation of Computerised Personal Data Files,[205] but they remained below the standards set forth in the Convention 108 and in any case were not binding instruments.

In 1990, seven out of twelve Member States had adopted legislation related to the protection of individuals vis-à-vis the processing of personal data and these legislations were diverging on a number of points.[206] The persistence of these divergences explained why the European Commission ultimately felt it necessary to propose the adoption of a Directive concerning the protection of individuals in relation to the processing of personal data. It is important here to understand that given the principle of conferred power, and thereby the specific allocation of competence between the European Community and Member States, the protection of fundamental rights of individuals could only be at that time an indirect consequence of the framework adopted. Indeed, the legal basis adopted for the Directive was ex-Article 95 of the

---

[199] See in particular Article 3.

[200] This is true in particular as regards sensitive data. See Article 6: "Personal data revealing racial origin, political opinions or religious or other beliefs, as well as personal data concerning health or sexual life, may not be processed automatically unless domestic law provides appropriate safeguards. The same shall apply to personal data relating to criminal convictions".

[201] Rec(87)15E 17 September 1987 regulating the use of personal data in the police sector.

[202] Additional Protocol to the Convention for the Protection of Individuals with regard to Automatic Processing of Personal Data regarding supervisory authorities and transborder data flows, Strasbourg, 8. XI.2001.

[203] See in particular Article 2.

[204] Recommendation of the Council concerning guidelines governing the protection of privacy and transborder flows of personal data (23 September 1980) followed by the 1985 Declaration on Transborder Data Flows and the 1998 Ministerial Declaration on the Protection of Privacy on Global Networks.

[205] Guidelines for the Regulation of Computerized Personal Data Files, G.A. res. 44/132, 44 U.N. GAOR Supp. (No. 49) at 211, U.N. Doc. A/44/49 (1989).

[206] For a presentation of Member states' regimes at the time of the adoption of the Directive 1995/47/EC see e.g. Mayer-Schönberger [22], Reidenberg [23], at S148–S164. See also Proposal for a Council Directive concerning the protection of individuals in relation to the processing of personal data 1990 COM(90) 314 final.

Treaty of the European Community [now Article 114 of the Treaty for the functioning of the European Union (TFEU), as introduced by the Lisbon Treaty] of which the final objective was/is the establishment and functioning of the internal market.[207] As a result, in this sense and in this sense only, data protection law was expressly meant to ease data processing.[208] This explains why the data protection Directive has been conceived as a measure of maximum harmonisation.[209]

Things have changed, however, with the adoption of the Lisbon Treaty. Article 16(1) TFEU now establishes the principle that everyone has the right to the protection of personal data concerning him or her. Above all, Article 16(2) TFEU introduces a specific legal basis for the adoption of rules on the protection of personal data: "[t]he European Parliament and the Council, acting in accordance with the ordinary legislative procedure, shall lay down the rules relating to the protection of individuals with regard to the processing of personal data by Union institutions, bodies, offices and agencies, and by the Member States when carrying out activities which fall within the scope of Union law, and the rules relating to the free movement of such data. Compliance with these rules shall be subject to the control of independent authorities". Although the rules relating to the protection of individuals and the rules relating to the free movement of such data are mentioned together, the rules relating to the protection of individuals now come first and are not anymore instrumentalised to serve the second. Besides are included within the scope of Article 16(1) rules on the protection for personal data that applies to judicial co-operation in criminal matters and police co-operation. Not only cross-border exchanges can be regulated on the ground of Article 16, but also mere national activities.

As regards the material scope of the data protection Directive 1995/48/EC[210], it is necessary to recall the following three points. The latter help to understand that data protection law has had an impact upon the evolution of the ECtHR's case law. First of all, the data protection Directive adopts a very broad definition of personal data:

---

[207] See also CJEU 28 March 1996 Opinion 2/94 Accession by the Community to the European Convention for the Protection of Human Rights and Fundamental Freedoms at [27]: "No Treaty provision confers on the Community institutions any general power to enact rules on human rights or to conclude international conventions in this field".

[208] See Serge Gutwirth, Raphael Gellert and Rocco Bellanova, VUB, Michael Friedewald and Philip Schütz, Fraunhofer ISI, David Wright, Trilateral Research & Consulting Emilio Mordini and Silvia Venier, Legal, social, economic and ethical conceptualisations of privacy and data protection, D1 Prescient research project, at http://prescient-project.eu/prescient/inhalte/download/PRESCIENT-D1—final.pdf (23 March 2011), p. 3–4, who oppose data protection law to Article 8 and state that the two bodies of law have distinct rationale. While I agree that data protection law had initially been conceived as a means to facilitate the free flow of information, the main difference lies in the nature of the regulatory strategy underlying the two bodies of rules. One is reactive, the other proactive.

[209] Confirmed by the CJEU in Lindqvist C-101/01 [2003] ECR I-12971 at [96] (Lindqvist): "[t]he harmonisation of those national laws is therefore not limited to minimal harmonisation but amounts to harmonisation which is generally complete. It is upon that view that Directive 95/46 is intended to ensure free movement of personal data while guaranteeing a high level of protection for the rights and interests of the individuals to whom such data relate".

[210] Council Directive 95/46/EC of 24 October 1995 on the protection of individuals with regard to the processing of personal data and on the free movement of such data [1995] OJ L281/31.

"'personal data' shall mean any information relating to an identified or identifiable natural person ('data subject')" and "an identifiable person"[211] is one who can be identified, "directly or indirectly, in particular by reference to an identification number or to one or more factors specific to his physical, physiological, mental, economic, cultural or social identity".[212] By "information", one has to understand not only written information but all type of information including aural and visual information.[213] Although nominative data are certainly included in the category of personal data, the latter category is definitely wider: as long as it is possible after reasonable efforts to create a link between the information at issue and an individual, the information is going to be considered as personal data.[214] Consequently, the category of personal data unsurprisingly goes beyond that of secret or confidential data and should include "Browser-Generated Information" (information exchanged between a user and a website through the means of a browser, e.g. the URL of a website).[215]

Second, as regards the processing of personal data, once again the definition adopted is very broad and thereby reflects or even anticipates the evolution of the ECtHR's case law. By "processing" one must thus understand "any operation or set of operations which is performed upon personal data, whether or not by automatic means, such as collection, recording, organisation, storage, adaptation or alteration, retrieval, consultation, use, disclosure by transmission, dissemination or otherwise making available, alignment or combination, blocking, erasure or destruction".[216] This is not an exhaustive inventory. Collection, storage and a fortiori misuses are mentioned. Notably the mere consultation amounts to a processing. As a result, the consultation of a website even without the storing of data would be tantamount to an act of processing.[217] This said, it is important to note that under Article 3(2), the data protection Directive "shall

---

[211] Legal persons are excluded from the scope of the protection for here we are only concerned about individuals.

[212] Article 2(a).

[213] See recital 14 of the data protection Directive.

[214] See recital 26: "to determine whether a person is identifiable, account should be taken of all the means likely reasonably to be used either by the controller or by any other person to identify the said person".

[215] What matters is whether the user browsing the web is identifiable. Vidal-Hall et al. v Google Inc. [2014] EWHC 13 (QB) at [117] (Vidal). There is a strong argument that the English case law up until Vidal has been too restrictive. See in particular Micheal John Durant v Financial Services Authority [2003] EWCA Civ 1746 and Lord and R (Department of Health) v Information Commissioner [2011] EWHC 1430 (Admin); Johnson v Medical Defence Union [2004] EWHC 347. In Durant Auld L.J. stated that "not all information retrieved from a computer search against an individual's name or unique identifier is personal data within the meaning of the Act". One could also argue M. Tugendhat's interpretation in Vidal of private information remains too narrow though.

[216] Article 2(b).

[217] In Lindqvist, the CJEU held at [25] that "[a]ccording to the definition in Article 2(b) of Directive 95/46, the term 'processing' of such data used in Article 3(1) covers 'any operation or set of operations which is performed upon personal data, whether or not by automatic means'. That provision gives several examples of such operations, including disclosure by transmission, dissemination or otherwise making data available. It follows that the operation of loading personal data on an Internet page must be considered to be such processing".

not apply to the processing of personal data… by a natural person in the course of a purely personal or household activity". Interestingly the proposed general data protection Regulation[218] has opted for a slightly more restrictive formulation: the regulation does not apply to the "processing of personal data … by a natural person without any gainful interest in the course of its own exclusively personal or household activity".[219]

Third, the person responsible for the processing, and who will have to abide by a certain number of duties, is the data controller who is "the natural or legal person, public authority, agency or any other body which alone or jointly with others determines the purposes and means of the processing of personal data".[220] The fact that the data controller has to determine both the purposes and the means of processing has rendered its identification quite complex in the context of Web 2.0 applications and in particular social networking websites[221] and of cloud computing.[222] In the context of complex relationships involving different actors, the criterion of who determines the finality of the processing seems nevertheless to be the conclusive factor.

On the whole, as regards the logic underlying the legal framework, it does echo that of the test embedded within Article 8 and its interpretation by the ECtHR although the remit of data protection law is broader as explained in Fig. 1.3. All processing of personal data, except those undertaken by a natural person in the course of a purely personal or household activity, is of concern. Nevertheless, they become legitimate when data controllers comply with the procedure and safeguards set up by the data protection Directive, and its transposition at the national level, acting as a legal basis within the meaning of the case law developed by the ECtHR.

---

[218] The European Commission, Proposal for a Regulation on the protection of individuals with regard to the processing of personal data and on the free movement of such data (General Data Protection Regulation), COM(2012) 11 Final.

[219] Article 2(2)(d). Recital 15 adds that "[t]he exemption should also not apply to controllers or processor which provide the means for processing personal data for such personal or domestic activities".

[220] Article 2(d).

[221] See the answer given by the Article 29 Working party Opinion 5/2009 on online social networking (12.06.2009) at p. 5 which states "SNS [Social Network Service] providers are data controllers under the Data Protection Directive. They provide the means for the processing of user data and provide all the 'basic' services related to user management (e.g. registration and deletion of accounts). SNS providers also determine the use that may be made of user data for advertising and marketing purposes—including advertising provided by third parties". Besides, "[a]pplication providers may also be data controllers, if they develop applications which run in addition to the ones from the SNS and users decide to use such an application". With regard to users, they are in most cases considered as mere data subjects because of the application of the household exemption. See more generally Opinion 1/2010 on the concepts of "controller" and "processor" (16.02.2010). The Article 29 Working Party has nevertheless a mere advisory status.

[222] See Article 29 Working Party Opinion 05/2012 on Cloud Computing (01.07.2012) at pp. 7–8 which states "[t]he cloud client determines the ultimate purpose of the processing and decides on the outsourcing of this processing and the delegation of all or part of the processing activities to an external organisation. The cloud client therefore acts as a data controller. … The cloud provider is the entity that provides the cloud computing services in the various forms discussed above. When the cloud provider supplies the means and the platform, acting on behalf of the cloud client, the cloud provider is considered as a data processor".

	Data protection Directive Proactive protection of private life interests	Article 8 ECHR Reactive protection of private life interests
1. Legitimate end	(a) the data subject has unambiguously given his consent; or (b) processing is necessary for the performance of a contract to which the data subject is party or in order to take steps at the request of the data subject prior to entering into a contract; or (c) processing is necessary for compliance with a legal obligation to which the controller is subject; or (d) processing is necessary in order to protect the vital interests of the data subject; or (e) processing is necessary for the performance of a task carried out in the public interest or in the exercise of official authority vested in the controller or in a third party to whom the data are disclosed; or (f) processing is necessary for the purposes of the legitimate interests pursued by the controller or by the third party or parties to whom the data are disclosed, except where such interests are overridden by the interests for fundamental rights and freedoms of the data subject which require protection under Article 1 (1). [Article 7] **NB 1:** It is arguable that these legitimate ends go beyond the protection of the rights and freedoms of the data collectors. It can therefore be sustained that they are too broad **NB 2:** Even if the data subject gives her consent, the processing must still be of quality and secure.	(a) national security, (b) public safety or the economic well-being of the country, (c) for the prevention of disorder or crime, (d) for the protection of health or morals, (e) or for the protection of the rights and freedoms of others. **NB:** Consent seems to be able to transform in certain cases the interference into a non-interference. "[T]he collection and storage of personal information relating to the applicant's telephone, as well as to her email and internet usage, without her knowledge, amounted to an interference with her right to respect for her private life and correspondence within the meaning of Art.8". [Copland].

Fig. 1.3 The complementarity of data protection law and Article 8 (ECHR)

2. In accordance with the law

2.1 Accessible legal basis

The data protection Directive and its transposition at the national level meet that criterion.

2.2 Foreseeable legal basis

The aim of the drafters of the Directive has been to allow data subjects to predict when a processing is undertaken in order to enable them to exercise control over it. However it is arguable whether the framework is entirely satisfactory. See the legitimate ends (e) and (f) which if interpreted broadly can be very far-reaching and thereby prevent data subjects to actually predict when a processing is undertaken.

3.2 Accessible legal basis

- "Firstly, the law must be adequately accessible: the citizen must be able to have an indication that is adequate in the circumstances of the legal rules applicable to a given case". [Sunday Times; Malone]

- "[T]he Court has always understood the term 'law' in its 'substantive' sense, not its 'formal' one; it has included both enactments of lower rank than statutes and unwritten law." [Kruslin; see also Sunday Times]

3.3 Foreseeable legal basis

- "Secondly, a norm cannot be regarded as 'law' unless it is formulated with sufficient precision to enable the citizen to regulate his conduct: he must be able—if need be with appropriate advice—to foresee, to a degree that is reasonable in the circumstances, the consequences which a given action may entail". [Sunday Times; Malone]

- "'[I]n accordance with the law' does not merely refer back to domestic law but also relates to the quality of the law, requiring it to be compatible with the rule of law, which is expressly mentioned in the preamble to the Convention. The phrase thus implies—and this follows from the object and purpose of Article 8—that there must be a measure of legal protection in domestic law against arbitrary interferences by public authorities with the rights safeguarded by paragraph 1" [Malone]

- "[T]he law must indicate the scope of any such discretion conferred on the competent authorities and the manner of its exercise with sufficient clarity ... to give the individual adequate protection against arbitrary interference". [Malone]

Fig. 1.3 (continued)

3. Necessary in a democratic society	Several safeguards have been set forth to ensure the proportionality of the processing, although it is arguable whether all are really effective. Among the several safeguards we find: • The data shall be collected for specified, explicit and legitimate purposes and not further processed in a way incompatible with those purposes [Article 6]. • The data shall be adequate, relevant and not excessive in relation to the purposes for which they are collected and/or further processed [Article 6]. • The data shall be accurate and, where necessary, kept up to date; every reasonable step must be taken to ensure that data which are inaccurate or incomplete, having regard to the purposes for which they were collected or for which they are further processed, are erased or rectified [Article 6]. • The data shall be kept in a form which permits identification of data subjects for no longer than is necessary for the purposes for which the data were collected or for which they are further processed [Article 6]. • The controller must implement appropriate technical and organizational measures to protect personal data against accidental or unlawful destruction or accidental loss, alteration, unauthorized disclosure or access, in particular where the processing involves the transmission of data over a network, and against all other unlawful forms of processing. [Article 17] • Data subject's right of information [Articles 10 & 11] • Data subject's right to access [Article 12] • Data subject's right tor rectification, erasure or blocking of data [Article 12] • Data subject's right to object [Article 14] • Data subject's right to a judicial remedy for any breach of the rights guaranteed by the national law applicable to the processing in question [Article 22] & Data subject's right to receive compensation for damage suffered as a result of an unlawful processing operation [Article 23] • Prior checking by national public authorities in cases in which the processing operations are likely to present specific risks [Article 20] • Publicity of processing operations [Article 20]	The court examines safeguards existing at the time of the interference and in particular weight is given to: • The purpose of the interference • Whether the interference is a measure of targeted or massive surveillance and thereby how the category of interferees is defined • The duration of the interference • The existence of any supervision to control the modalities of the interference • The rights of the interferee as regards the information collected (right to access, right to verify, right to ask for the erasure) • As regards interferences by the police, whether a judge has authorized the interference

Fig. 1.3 (continued)

The legal basis set forth by the data protection Directive seems in several respects less stringent than what the ECtHR would require under Article 8(2). But this is comprehensible for the data protection Directive predates the evolution of the ECtHR's case law and the majority view at that time was for legitimate reasons that data protection law was in reality far wider in scope than traditional privacy law. In addition, and this is crucial to understand the interplay between the protection of the right to respect for private life and data protection law, one important difference between the data protection Directive and Article 8 relates to the regulatory strategy underlying the legal provisions.[223] The data protection Directive has been conceived by its drafters as a proactive regulatory instrument intended to frame, at the stage at which the decision to process is to be taken, the behaviour of public and private actors acting as data controllers.

In this line, the provision relating to the obligation to notify the Data protection Agency of the processing (Article 18) is based upon the assumption that generally speaking processing should be transparent so that an assessment of its appropriateness is possible at an early stage either at the initiative of data subjects or the supervisory authority. Notably though, the proposed general data protection Regulation has dropped the requirement of notification.[224]

The drafters of the Directive have thus elaborated a far-reaching framework with an open list of exceptions to be found in Article 13 for purposes of (a) national security; (b) defence; (c) public security; (d) the prevention, investigation, detection and prosecution of criminal offences, or of breaches of ethics for regulated professions; (e) an important economic or financial interest of a Member State or of the European Union, including monetary, budgetary and taxation matters; (f) a monitoring, inspection or regulatory function connected, even occasionally, with the exercise of official authority in cases referred to in (c), (d) and (e); (g) the protection of the data subject or of the rights and freedoms of others.

They also set forth a relatively "generous" list of legitimising ends not to burden too much businesses, who should be able to freely pursue at least the core of their business purposes.[225] It might be thought that the list of legitimising ends is in fact too generous since it includes "the performance of a task carried out in the public interest or in the exercise of official authority vested in the controller or in a third party to whom the data are disclosed"; and above all the "pursuance of legitimate interests by the controller or by the third party or parties to whom the data are disclosed, except where such interests are overridden by the interests for fundamental rights and freedoms of the data subject which require protection under Article 1 (1)".

---

[223] This is not to deny that both the provisions of the data protection Directive and Article 8 of the ECHR can have ex ante and ex post effects. I am just trying to highlight the regulatory strategy underlying the data protection Directive which differs from that of Article 8 of the ECHR.

[224] It, however, includes demanding record keeping obligations. See Article 22, 28.

[225] It is worth mentioning that under UK law (SI 2000/188) processing for staff administration, processing for advertising marketing and public relations and processing for accounts and record keeping do not require prior notification to the Information Commissioner. This does not mean that data controllers do not have to comply with the rest of the Data Protection Act of 1998.

As a result, and because of its proactive stance, the data protection Directive cannot be conceived as direct implementation of Article 8, although it is definitely an attempt to regulate and thereby constrain profiling activities. It is thus a complementary instrument of public regulation meant to primarily have a deterrent effect.

In view of the evolution of the ECtHR's case law, it should nevertheless be clear that each time a dimension of surveillance is at stake in the processing of personal data, Article 8 is potentially applicable on top of data protection law and will make the scrutiny of the surveillance measure possible. Obviously, surveillance goes beyond police activity. At the same time, a wide range of personal data processing as covered by the data protection Directive has implications in terms of the right to the protection of private life, albeit modest.

Besides, when the ECtHR has to scrutinise a surveillance measure, it needs to check whether the activity of public interest pursues at least one of the following legitimate ends: (a) national security, (b) public safety or the economic well-being of the country, (c) the prevention of disorder or crime, (d) the protection of health or morals and (e) the protection of the rights and freedoms of others. Above all, the ECtHR needs to determine whether the legal basis is of quality and whether the surveillance measure implemented in compliance with this legal basis is necessary in a democratic society. The proportionality of the measure at stake relying upon the processing of personal data and thereby its effectiveness has thus to be assessed at this stage.

This is this precise enquiry which could potentially target data protection legislation that justifies making the right to respect for private life a higher norm than the right to the protection of personal data as illustrated by Fig. 1.4.

In this regard, the last category of legitimising end to be found in Article 7 of the data protection Directive is maybe the most problematic ("when the processing is necessary for the purposes of the legitimate interests pursued by the controller or by the third party or parties to whom the data are disclosed, except where such interests are overridden by the interests for fundamental rights and freedoms of the data subject which require protection"…). Indeed, the data protection Directive balances two undetermined notions: the interest of the data controller and the interest of the data subject. This is all the more problematic that in practice this legitimising end is often invoked by data controllers.

Fig. 1.4 The hierarchy of norms

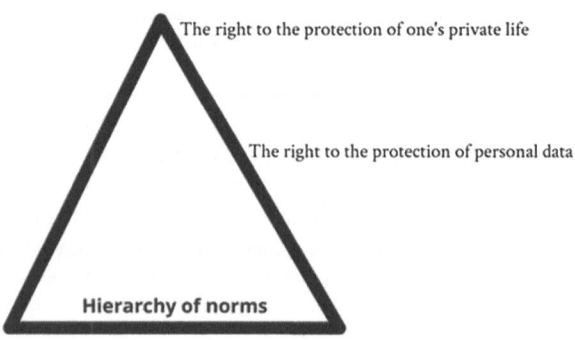

The right to the protection of one's private life

The right to the protection of personal data

Hierarchy of norms

In addition, what is important to note for our purpose is the way the material scope of the framework laid down has been delineated in the data protection Directive. Article 3(2) echoing Article 13 provides that "[t]his Directive shall not apply to ... processing operations concerning public security, defence, State security (including the economic well-being of the State when the processing operation relates to State security matters) and the activities of the State in areas of criminal law".[226] This exclusion is far from being obvious for ex-Article 95 [now Article 114 of TFEU], on which the adoption of the Directive had been grounded, had always been far-reaching as long as the measure was adopted for the purpose of establishing and ensuring the functioning of the internal market. But, the inclusion of such an exclusion leaving some of the most serious privacy threats outside of the reach of the harmonised legal framework shows the limits of European harmonisation when primarily centred on the paradigm of economic integration.[227]

In the end, given the shortcoming of the data protection Directive, Article 8 of the ECHR remains crucial to ensure not too much processing of personal data is taking place.

Before looking at the sectorial measures of harmonisation, it is worth mentioning the proposed Regulation intended to fill the gaps of the data protection Directive and offer a comprehensive set of common rules. The proposed Regulation, which enriches the list of safeguards in particular by awarding data subjects new or more comprehensive rights such as the right to data portability,[228] the right to be forgotten and to erasure,[229] the right to receive data breach notification,[230] goes one step further towards the adoption of the criteria used by the ECtHR to assess the legitimacy of interferences to Article 8(1). In Article 7(3), one can read that as regards the last four legitimising ends "the law of the Member State must meet an objective of public interest or must be necessary to protect the rights and freedoms of others, respect the essence of the right to the protection of personal data and be proportionate to the legitimate end pursued".

Moreover, interestingly Article 7(2) provides that "consent shall not provide a legal basis for the processing, where there is a significant imbalance between the

---

[226] It is not clear whether the formulation adopted by the proposed general data Regulation will be interpreted in a more restrictive manner. See Article 2 about the material scope of the Regulation.

[227] However, some shared minimum standards existed for all Member States had ratified the Convention 108 and the Council of Europe had adopted a sectorial recommendation to regulate personal data processing by the police. Recommendation R (87).

[228] Article 17.

[229] Article 18.

[230] Article 32. The language of rights is not used in this article tough. This said it goes beyond Article 20 of the data protection Directive which simply requires Member States to "determine the processing operations likely to present specific risks to the rights and freedoms of data subjects and (...) check that these processing operations are examined prior to the start thereof". In the UK, this provision has not been fully implemented. Section 22 of the Data Protection Act of 1998 does grant the Secretary of State the power to determine categories of assessable processing but so far no determination has been made.

position of the data subject and the controller". Consent is thus losing its legitimising power, which echoes the recent definition of private life put forward by the ECtHR.

Finally, Article 33 of the proposed general data protection Regulation expressly identifies processing operations that present specific risks and which should require the data controller to consult the supervisory authority prior to the processing.[231] In this list are included: "(a) a systematic and extensive evaluation of personal aspects relating to a natural person or for analysing or predicting in particular the natural person's economic situation, location, health, personal preferences, reliability or behaviour, which is based on automated processing and on which measures are based that produce legal effects concerning the individual or significantly affect the individual; (b) information on sex life, health, race and ethnic origin or for the provision of health care, epidemiological researches, or surveys of mental or infectious diseases, where the data are processed for taking measures or decisions regarding specific individuals on a large scale; (c) monitoring publicly accessible areas, especially when using optic-electronic devices (video surveillance) on a large scale; (d) personal data in large-scale filing systems on children, genetic data or biometric data; (e) other processing operations for which the consultation of the supervisory authority is required pursuant to point (b) of Article 34(2)". Nevertheless, the initiative of the consultation must come from the data controller. More importantly, data protection impact assessments are not meant to assess the effectiveness of the measures relying upon the processing of personal data and thereby to determine whether less costly alternatives are available.

On the whole though, Article 7 and 33 of the proposed Regulation do not render Article 8 useless. Even with the adoption of the proposed Regulation, Article 8 of the ECHR remains crucial to ensure not too much processing of personal data is taking place.

1.3.2 Processing by the Police

The European Commission has recently proposed the adoption of a Directive on the protection of individuals with regard to the processing of personal data by competent authorities for the purposes of prevention, investigation, detection or prosecution of criminal offences or the execution of criminal penalties, and the free movement of such data[232] which builds upon the Framework Decision

---

[231] Article 34(2).

[232] Proposal for a Directive of the European Parliament and of The Council on the protection of individuals with regard to the processing of personal data by competent authorities for the purposes of prevention, investigation, detection or prosecution of criminal offences or the execution of criminal penalties, and the free movement of such data COM/2012/010 final—2012/0010 (COD).

2008/977/JHA.[233] Indeed, the creation of an "Area of Freedom, Security and Justice"[234] at the European level after that of an internal market, made it necessary to enhance the quality and quantity of exchanges of information between Member States. As a result, harmonisation in the field of data protection law was felt a necessity as well as the need to secure compliance with the principle of availability of information.[235] While the free flow of information seems to be the prevailing raison d'être of such a regime, the Commission opined in 2005 that "[a] legal instrument on common standards for the protection of personal data processed for the purpose of preventing and combating crime should be consistent with the overall policy of the European Union in the area of privacy and data protection. Wherever possible, taking into account the necessity of improving the efficiency of legitimate activities of the police, customs, judicial and other competent authorities, it should therefore follow existing and proven principles and definitions, notably those laid down in Directive 95/46/EC of the European Parliament and of the Council or relating to the exchange of information by Europol, Eurojust, or processed via the Customs Information System or other comparable instruments".[236]

This proposed Directive is one of the two instruments comprising the new legal framework for the protection of personal data in the EU, as presented by the Commission in 2012.[237] Its structure thus resembles that of the data protection Directive and thereby indirectly mirrors that of Article 8: one finds a list of legitimate ends and a list of safeguards that are meant to appropriately calibrate the processing to the end pursued.

---

[233] Council Framework Decision 2008/977/JHA on the protection of personal data processed in the framework of police and judicial cooperation in criminal matters OJ L 350, 30.12.2008 pp. 60–71. This framework Decision has a limited scope of application, since it only applies to cross-border data processing. Besides, it gives Member States a large leeway to implement its provisions. And, it does not contain provisions relating to supervision by an advisory group similar to the Article 29 Working Party or oversight by the European Commission to ensure a common approach in its implementation. See also Council Framework Decision 2006/960/JHA of 18 December 2006 on simplifying the exchange of information and intelligence between law enforcement authorities of the Member States of the European Union OJ L 386, 29.12.2006, pp. 89–100.

[234] The creation of the area of freedom, security and justice is based on the Tampere (1999–04), Hague (2004–09) and Stockholm (2010–14) programmes. It derives from Title V of the TFEU, which regulates the "Area of freedom, security and justice".

[235] See 29 March 2004 COM(2004) 221; 16 June 2004 COM(2004) 429; Proposal for a Council framework decision on the protection of personal data processed in the framework of police and judicial co-operation in criminal matters COM(2005) 475; COM(2005) 490.

[236] Proposal for a Council framework decision on the protection of personal data processed in the framework of police and judicial co-operation in criminal matters COM(2005) 475 Recital 6.

[237] Communication from the Commission to the European Parliament, the Council, the European Economic and Social Committee and the Committee of the Regions safeguarding privacy in a connected world—A European data protection framework for the 21st Century COM(2012) 9 final.

The proposed Directive contains some interesting provisions. In particular is to be welcome the recognition of a right to access[238] which implies the recognition of a right to request that the supervisory authority checks the lawfulness of the processing.[239] In addition, the needs of a democratic society are taken into account to assess the legitimacy of the measures adopted to restrict the right to information and the right to access. By way of example, Article 13(1) provides that "[m]ember States may adopt legislative measures restricting, wholly or partly, the data subject's right of access to the extent that such partial or complete restriction constitutes a necessary and proportionate measure in a democratic society with due regard for the legitimate interests of the person concerned: (a) to avoid obstructing official or legal inquiries, investigations or procedures; (b) to avoid prejudicing the prevention, detection, investigation and prosecution of criminal offences or the execution of criminal penalties; (c) to protect public security; (d) to protect national security; (e) to protect the rights and freedoms of others". That being said, this enquiry is only relevant for measures restricting the right to information and the right to access, and not for assessing the legitimacy of the processing in general.

Nevertheless, the list of legitimising ends is once again largely open, although the European Commission appears to have sifted the legitimising ends of Article 7 of the data protection Directive.[240] Besides, the prohibition to process special categories of personal data, such as personal data revealing race or ethnic origin, political opinions, religion or beliefs, trade union membership, genetic data or data concerning health or sex life, to be found in Article 8(1), is directly undermined by Article 8(2), which provides that Member States do not have an obligation to prohibit the processing of special categories of personal data where "the processing is authorised by a law providing appropriate safeguards".

Finally, the proposed Directive does not force Member States to expressly distinguish between measures of targeted surveillance and measures of mass surveillance with the view of setting forth more stringent rules for the latter category. Truly Article 5 obliges Member States, to the extent possible, to make controllers distinguish between personal data of different categories of data subjects such as: "persons with regard to whom there are serious grounds for believing that they have committed or are about to commit a criminal offence; (b) persons convicted of a criminal offence; (c) victims of a criminal offence, or persons with regard to whom certain facts give reasons for believing that he or she could be the victim of a criminal offence; (d) third parties to the criminal offence, such as persons who

---

[238] Articles 12 to 14. There is also a right to information (Article 11 & Article 29), a right to rectification (Article 15) and a right to erasure (Article 15). The right to access is already included in the Framework Decision 2008/977/JHA, but its modalities of exercise such as the right to request an assessment of the lawfulness of the processing are not regulated. See Article 17 of the Framework Decision 2008/977/JHA.

[239] Article 14.

[240] "The other grounds for lawful processing in Article 7 of Directive 95/46/EC are not appropriate for the processing in the area of police and criminal justice" states the Commission in COM(2012) 10 final, p. 7.

might be called on to testify in investigations in connection with criminal offences or subsequent criminal proceedings, or a person who can provide information on criminal offences, or a contact or associate to one of the persons mentioned in (a) and (b); and (e) persons who do not fall within any of the categories referred to above".[241] Such a provision does not necessarily guarantee that no issue of foreseeability of the legal basis can arise and a fortiori issues of proportionality in relation to the duration of the retention of the personal data or the seriousness of the offence to be prosecuted or prevented.

The fate of the proposal for a Directive on the protection of individuals with regard to the processing of personal data by competent authorities for the purposes of prevention, investigation, detection or prosecution of criminal offences or the execution of criminal penalties, and the free movement of such data will, however, depend upon the reaction of the EU legislator to the declaration of the invalidity of the data retention Directive pronounced by the CJEU on 8 April 2014.[242]

All in all, what this proposed piece of legislation shows though, despite its defects, is the "relative" influence of the framework developed by the ECtHR to assess the legitimacy of surveillance measures. However, when national security is at stake and not simply the prevention, investigation, detection or prosecution of criminal offences or the execution of criminal penalties, Member States[243] regain a substantial leeway, as we then fall outside the scope of Union law. The possibility to resort to the ECtHR is thus de nuovo essential to confine surveillance activities. This is all the more true that under Klass, an applicant to the ECtHR does not always have to prove that the surveillance measures impugned were in fact applied to her. To cite the ECtHR, an "individual may, under certain conditions, claim to be the victim of a violation occasioned by the mere existence of secret measures or of legislation permitting secret measures, without having to allege that such measures were in fact applied to him".[244]

By way of example, in the UK, the Data Protection Act of 1998 provides a wide exemption for the processing of personal data when such an exemption is necessary to safeguard national security (Section 28). No definition of what amounts to safeguarding national security is specified in the Act. And any data controller can claim it. RIPA 2000 remains, however, applicable in as much as the interception takes place in the UK.[245] RIPA 2000 distinguishes between "internal" and "external" communi-

---

[241] This is a new provision which was neither present in the data protection Directive nor in the Framework Decision 2008/977/JHA. However, it finds its roots in the Council of Europe's Recommendation No R (87)15. See also Euoropol Decision 2009/371/JHA (Article 14) and Eurojust Decision 2009/426/JHA (Article 15).

[242] See infra pp. 63–64

[243] See Article 13 of the data protection Directive and Article 2 of the proposed general data protection Regulation. Note that in the proposed general data protection Regulation article 13 has disappeared though which limits the range of exceptions that Member States can carve out.

[244] Klass at [34]. See also Weber at [78] and Liberty at [56–57].

[245] The Guardian and the Washington Post have also revealed that the UK authorities have asked the US agency (NSA) to supply data intercepted or accessed to in the US. In this case RIPA 2000 is not applicable.

cations. When the communication is internal,[246] an (interception) warrant must authorise the interception and identify the interception subject or a single set of premises for which the interception is to take place.[247] In Kennedy,[248] as aforementioned, the ECtHR held that for internal communications the legal basis (RIPA 2000 and the Interception of Communications Code of Practice) was satisfactory for the purposes of Article 8(2). The Tempora programme described as relying upon the interception of more than 200 fibre-optic cables landing in the UK is nevertheless likely to fall afoul of Article 8 in as much as it does not seem to have been implemented "in accordance with the law". Tempora appears to have been authorised under certificated warrants issued under Section 8(4) of RIPA 2000. Yet, Section 8(4) applicable in principle only to external communications simply requires the Secretary of State to certify that the intercepted materials are necessary in the interests of national security. The interception subject or the set of premises for which the interception is to take place do not have to be described. More importantly, if one follows Liberty, the conditions for selecting information (to be read or listened to), storing, sharing, accessing and destroying intercepted material are not clearly stated. The proportionality of the surveillance measure is also a problem, assuming the interception or monitoring is used indiscriminately against private citizens and suspects and the information can be transmitted to other governmental organs without further checks.[249]

The processing of personal data for the purposes of the prevention or detection of crime or the apprehension or prosecution of offender is not excluded from the scope of the UK Data Protection Act, although it is exempt from the first data protection principle (principle of fairness)[250] and Section 7 concerning the right to access. As aforementioned, RIPA 2000 is also applicable. Part II of RIPA 2000 is relevant when the processing of personal data is used as a method of directed surveillance or intrusive surveillance and requires prior (administrative) authorisation.[251] Whereas intrusive surveillance is very limited in scope (covert surveillance carried out in relation to anything taking place on any residential premises or in any private vehicle and involving the presence of an individual on the premises or in the vehicle or carried out by means of a surveillance device),[252] directed surveillance is defined more broadly:

---

[246] Under s.20 of RIPA 2000, "external communication" means a communication sent or received outside the British Islands.

[247] Section 8(1). See also Section 8(2) and (3) concerning information relating to the apparatus to be used and the communication to be intercepted.

[248] Kennedy at [169–170].

[249] It is reported that "[f]ull content of transmissions is preserved for 3 days and metadata for 30" in P. Bump, The UK Tempora Program Captures Vast Amounts of Data—and Shares with NSA, The Wire, 21 June 2013, http://www.thewire.com/national/2013/06/uk-tempora-program/66490/. See also the statements of grounds submitted before the Investigatory Powers Tribunal by Privacy International on 8 July 2013, https://www.privacyinternational.org/sites/privacyinternational.org/files/downloads/press-releases/privacy_international_ipt_grounds.pdf.

[250] Except to the extent to which it requires compliance with the conditions in Schedules 2 and 3.

[251] Section 27 RIPA 2000.

[252] Section 26(3) RIPA 2000.

covert surveillance carried for the purposes of "a specific investigation or a specific operation"; and "in such a manner as is likely to result in the obtaining of private information about a person (whether or not one specifically identified for the purposes of the investigation or operation)"; and otherwise than by way of an immediate response to events or circumstances making it unreasonable to ask for prior authorisation. Generally speaking, Section 48(2) of RIPA 2000 specifies that surveillance includes the "monitoring, observing or listening to persons, their movements, their conversations or their other activities or communications" as well as the "recording [of] anything monitored, observed or listened to in the course of surveillance".

In the light of the ECtHR' case law, it should be clear that the surveillance of social networking websites relying upon the systematic or permanent recording of personal information to be found in the public domain should comply with adequate legal safeguards and therefore one could argue that at least prior authorisation is required within the meaning of Part II of RIPA 2000.[253] Going further it is dubious that the normative framework including the Data protection Act and RIPA 2000 meant to confine surveillance activities by the police is really satisfactory. No piece of legislation or code of practice clarifies the criteria for selecting, storing, sharing, accessing and destroying the personal data collected. Indeed, the Data Protection Act says very little in this regard and the Code of Practice on Covert Surveillance and Property Interference as revised in 2010 is of no help. In the end, the only technique that might legitimately escape Article 8 scrutiny is social media analytics as long as no personal data are collected.

Hence, the importance of Article 8 scrutiny not so much to prohibit the processing by the police when there is legitimate ground to do so but to make sure procedural safeguards are in place so that effective supervision can take place.

1.3.3 Processing by Providers of Electronic Communications Services

Data protection law has been examined so far without taking into account the role played by a category of key private actors within the information society: Internet and online service providers or, to use another label which does not fully overlap with the latter providers of publicly available electronic communications services or public electronic communications network. This is where the legal framework starts to leak.

Because providers of electronic communications services are private actors, their activities are in principle regulated by the data protection Directive. But the data protection Directive has to be combined with an additional instrument that has been adopted to take into account the specificities of the sector: the e-privacy Directive

---

[253] This is not a consensual interpretation and it does seem that in practice law-enforcement officers do not agree with such a finding for they argue that private life for the purposes of the application of RIPA 2000 differs from the ECtHR's understanding of private life. It is also to be noted that in England a violation of the right to respect for private life does not necessarily render the evidence inadmissible.

2002/58/EC.[254] The e-privacy Directive does not override the data protection Directive in the field of electronic communications. A contrario reasoning must thus be banned to interpret the provisions of the e-privacy Directive. Indeed, "Directive 95/46/EC applies ...to all matters concerning protection of fundamental rights and freedoms, which are not specifically covered by the provisions of this Directive, including the obligations on the controller and the rights of individuals". To be more precise under Article 1(2) of the e-privacy Directive "[t]he provisions of this Directive particularise and complement Directive 95/46/EC for the purposes mentioned in paragraph 1".

As regards the material scope of the e-privacy Directive, it applies to providers of publicly available services or public electronic communications networks only.[255] Interestingly, it is added that legal persons are also protected for the Directive "provide for protection of the legitimate interests of subscribers who are legal persons".[256] Article 89 of the proposed general data protection Regulation, however, provides for the deletion of this sentence.[257]

As aforementioned, under Article 7 of the data protection Directive, the processing becomes legitimate if it is necessary for the purposes of the legitimate interests pursued by the data controller. When it comes to providers of publicly available electronic communication services or public electronic communications networks, this means in particular that they can process traffic data for the purposes of subscriber billing and interconnection payments.[258] But this is one particular hypothesis and other legitimate interests can be characterised. In this line, Article 6(5) of the e-privacy Directive also mentions traffic management and fraud detection.

Another legitimate interest is identified in the proposed general data protection Regulation. This is where security interests, but this time both private and public security interests, step in to justify the processing. Indeed, one can read in recital 39 that "[t]he processing of data to the extent strictly necessary for the purposes of ensuring network and information security, i.e. the ability of a network or an information system to resist, at a given level of confidence, accidental events or unlawful or malicious actions that compromise the availability, authenticity, integrity

---

[254] Directive 2002/58/EC of the European Parliament and of the Council of 12 July 2002 concerning the processing of personal data and the protection of privacy in the electronic communications sector (Directive on privacy and electronic communications) OJ L 201, 31.7.2002, p. 37 amended two times by Directive 2006/24/EC of the European Parliament and the of the Council of 15 March 2006 and Directive 2009/136/EC of the European Parliament and of the Council of 25 November 2009.

[255] Article 3.

[256] Article 1(2).

[257] Indeed, Recital 12 of the proposed Regulation states that "[t]he protection afforded by this Regulation concerns natural persons, whatever their nationality or place of residence, in relation to the processing of personal data. With regard to the processing of data which concern legal persons and in particular undertakings established as legal persons, including the name and the form of the legal person and the contact details of the legal person, the protection of this Regulation should not be claimed by any person. This should also apply where the name of the legal person contains the names of one or more natural persons.".

[258] Article 6(2) of the e-privacy Directive: "Traffic data necessary for the purposes of subscriber billing and interconnection payments may be processed. Such processing is permissible only up to the end of the period during which the bill may be lawfully challenged or payment pursued".

and confidentiality of stored or transmitted data, and the security of the related services offered by, or accessible via, these networks and systems, by public authorities, Computer Emergency Response Teams (CERTs), Computer Security Incident Response Teams (CSIRTs), providers of electronic communications networks and services and by providers of security technologies and services, constitutes a legitimate interest of the concerned data controller". Some examples are given and concern mainly the prevention of criminal activities: the foregoing could "include preventing unauthorised access to electronic communications networks and malicious code distribution and stopping 'denial of service' attacks and damage to computer and electronic communication systems". Remarkably, the means used to pursue these security interests can imply a large amount of processing.[259]

Even more, most Internet and online service providers will, if the proposal for a Directive concerning measures to ensure a high common level of network and information security across the Union is adopted,[260] have in fact an obligation to take appropriate technical and organisational measures to manage the risk posed to the security of the networks and information systems which they control and use in their operations,[261] to the exception of micro-, small- and medium-sized enterprises.[262] However, it is not clear whether control over preventive forms of processing undertaken for guaranteeing the security of networks will ever take place. National competent authorities on the security of network and information systems to be set up under Article 6 of the proposed Directive have for their main job to receive notifications of security incidents. They are thus supposed to intervene once the security threat is looming (i.e. a risk)[263] or real.

---

[259] Router providers have recently taken the initiative to develop pro-active technologies primarily to increase the security of their systems and networks. However, interestingly while these technologies are intended to monitor traffic from users' home network to the Internet and block access to infectious programs, they can occasionally be used to detect and react upon or prevent alleged unlawful content. A new generation of "precautionary" intermediaries is thus emerging which develop security technologies that rely on systematic data collection and information blocking mechanisms both to secure their systems and networks and combat cybercrimes. See e.g. http://www.neowin.net/news/cisco-locks-users-out-of-their-routers-requires-invasive-cloud-service.

[260] Proposal for a Directive of the European Parliament and of the Council concerning measures to ensure a high common level of network and information security across of the Union COM(2013) 48 final.

[261] Article 14 of the proposed Directive. Market operators include "provider[s] of information society services which enable the provision of other information society services" (under Article 3).

[262] See Article 14 of the proposal for a Directive concerning measures to ensure a high common level of network and information security across the Union. Service providers targeted by the e-privacy Directive and Directive 2002/21/EC of the European Parliament and of the Council of 7 March 2002 on common regulatory framework for electronic communications networks and services ("Framework Directive") (see Article 4 and Article 13a, respectively) are already under such obligations. There is thus over time an extension of the scope of security obligations. The protection of the network has become a major concern and is distinct from that of the protection of personal data. Compare with Article 17 of the data protection Directive.

[263] Under Article 3(3) risk is defined as "any circumstance or event having a potential adverse effect on security".

To go on with the list of legitimising ends to be found in the e-privacy Directive, if the consent of the subscriber or user to whom the traffic data relates is obtained, the service provider can process the data for the purpose of marketing electronic communications services or for the provision of value-added services.[264] By value-added services, one must understand, namely "advice on least expensive tariff packages, route guidance, traffic information, weather forecasts and tourist information".[265] Because this time the user or subscriber consent is necessary to legitimise the processing, its duration depends upon the will of the user or subscriber: "[u]sers or subscribers shall be given the possibility to withdraw their consent for the processing of traffic data at any time".[266] But at the same time, as long as the user or subscriber does not withdraw her consent, the processing is likely to go on.

Because consent can be obtained quite easily and because the list of legitimate interests is not closed, the e-privacy Directive in reality opens the door to a large amount of processing. Importantly, the development of sophisticated profiling tools is eased by the possibility for the aforementioned service providers to process content data, as long as they respect the confidentiality of communications.[267] Yet, there is an argument that if interception of communication "takes place for purposes connected with the provision or operation of [a telecommunications service] or with the enforcement, in relation to that service, of any enactment relating to the use of postal services or telecommunications services" it is lawful.[268] Besides, it could also be sustained by some that confidentiality of communications needs to be understood differently in cyberspace where Internet and online service providers do need to inspect the different types of packet headers as well as application data in some cases to detect threats to the security of the network.

Truly, after the adoption of Directive 2009/36/EC[269], the processing of content data which implies the storing of information, or the gaining of access to information already stored, in the terminal equipment of a subscriber or user (i.e. by using cookies) can only be done after having obtained the consent of the user or subscriber. But this is so as long as the processing is not undertaken for the sole purpose of providing the service and when the information is stored on the user or subscriber's equipment.

In any case, once consent has been given, all types of content data can be processed.

---

[264] Article 6(3) of the e-privacy Directive.

[265] Recital 18 of the e-privacy Directive. Customers' enquiries in general should probably be part of the category of value-added services, although Art. 6(5) seems to distinguish between them.

[266] Article 6(3) of the e-privacy Directive.

[267] See Article 5 of the e-privacy Directive.

[268] RIPA 2000 s.3(3).

[269] Directive 2009/136/EC of the European Parliament and of the Council Of 25 November 2009 amending Directive 2002/22/EC on universal service and users' rights relating to electronic communications networks and services, Directive 2002/58/EC concerning the processing of personal data and the protection of privacy in the electronic communications sector and Regulation(EC) No 2006/2004 on cooperation between national authorities responsible for the enforcement of consumer protection laws, OJ L337/11, 18.12.2009, pp.11–36.

In the end, the e-privacy Directive does not appear to be more restrictive than the data protection Directive. On the contrary, processing of both traffic data and content data seems to be facilitated. Article 8 thus remains crucial to scrutinise the appropriateness of the profiling activities allowed, in particular when back doors are open to law-enforcement agencies.

1.4 Privacy and Data Retention

One moves further away from the needs of a democratic society with the Data retention Directive of 2006.[270] This has been recently confirmed by the CJEU on 8 April 2014.[271] Because the fate of national transpositions is unclear it is important to explain the interplay between privacy and data retention law.

Up until the decision of invalidity of the CJEU, the data retention Directive was aiming at making sure Member States impose upon providers of publicly available communications services or of public communications networks an obligation to retain data which are generated or processed by them (i.e. traffic data and location[272] data), in order to ensure that the data are available for the purpose of the investigation, detection and prosecution of serious crime for a period of at least 6 months and for not more than 2 years after the date of the communication.[273] The notion of serious crime is not defined by the drafters of the Directive: Member States remain competent to define such a notion.[274]

The justification for such an obligation of retention is to be found in Recital 11 of the Directive: "given the importance of traffic and location data for the investigation, detection, and prosecution of criminal offences, as demonstrated by research and the practical experience of several Member States, there is need to ensure at European level that data that are generated or processed, in the course of the supply of communications services, by providers of public available electronic communications services or of a public communications network are retained for a certain period, subject to the conditions provided for in this Directive".

---

[270] Directive 2006/24/EC of the European Parliament and of the Council of 15 March 2006 on the retention of data generated or processed in connection with the provision of publicly available electronic communications services or of public communications networks and amending Directive 2002/58/EC OJ L 105, 13/04/2006 pp. 54–63. Interestingly, data retention obligations are not present in US law. As service providers do retain data and there is not a comprehensive data protection law, data retention obligations are in fact not really needed.

[271] CJEU Joined cases C-393/12 and C-594/12 Digital Rights Ireland Ltd v Minister for Communications, Marin and Natural Resources et al. and Kärntner Landesregierung, Micheal Seitlinger, Christof Tschohl and others of 8 April 2014 (Digital Rights Ireland).

[272] Which arguably are also traffic data within the meaning of the e-privacy Directive, Article 9.

[273] Article 6 of the data retention Directive.

[274] Article 1(1) of the data retention Directive.

As a result of the data retention Directive, the requirement of consent[275] for processing traffic data and location data other than traffic data to be found in Article 6 and Article 9 of the e-privacy Directive had become an empty shell. It is true that in principle, the data retained can only be used for the purposes aforementioned. However, issues of accessibility, foreseeability and proportionality in the sense of the ECtHR's case law do emerge and explain the decision of the CJEU.

First, the notion of serious crime is not defined and the retention is to be undertaken in a systematic manner to target all subscribers and users. One could argue though that serious crimes are now identified at the European level for Article 83 of the TFEU lists particularly serious crimes with a cross-border dimension: terrorism, trafficking in human beings and sexual exploitation of women and children, illicit drug trafficking, illicit arms trafficking, money laundering, corruption, counterfeiting of means of payment, computer crime and organised crime.

Second, nothing is said about the procedure to follow for storing, sharing, accessing and destroying these data which remains of the competence of Member States.[276] Yet under Weber, these safeguards seem to be essential.

Third, the scope rationae personae of the Directive is both very broad and unclear. All ISPs' subscribers are concerned by the monitoring. In addition, it is not sure whether over-the-top service providers should not also be bound by such data retention obligations. Although the Open Systems Interconnect (OSI) model has been replaced by the TCP/IP networking model some years ago, Lukas Feiler convincingly argues that the category of providers of publicly available electronic communications services and of public electronic communications networks is in fact more limited than the category of intermediary "information society service providers" to be found in the e-commerce Directive.[277] "In the context of the [retention] Directive, the most important question is whether only Internet access providers or also other providers (like mail service providers) provide an 'electronic communications service'. Framework Directive article 2(c) requires that the service wholly or mainly consist in 'the conveyance of signals on electronic communications networks.' With respect to the Internet this definition only matches Internet access providers. Their service consists in the 'conveyance of signals' without any editorial control. Technically speaking, they provide services on the first three layers of the OSI Model: the physical layer, the data link layer, and the network layer".[278] Furthermore, "[s]ervices provided over the Internet (as opposed to service providing

---

[275] And more broadly the system of legitimizing ends to be found in the data protection Directive.

[276] The proposed Directive on the protection of individuals with regard to the processing of personal data by competent authorities for the purposes of prevention, investigation, detection or prosecution of criminal offences or the execution of criminal penalties, and the free movement of such data seems to be a bit more prescriptive though.

[277] See Article 12–14 of the Council Directive 2000/31/EC of 8 June 2000 on certain legal aspects of information society services, in particular electronic commerce, in the Internal Market [2000] OJ L178/1.

[278] Feiler [24], at 2–3 (Feiler).

access to the Internet) do not mainly consist 'in the conveyance of signals'—that is
something left to Internet access providers. Services provided over the Internet use
the last (or topmost) four layers of the OSI networking model: the application layer,
the presentation layer, the session layer, and the transport layer. They do not concern
themselves with the first three layers of the OSI Model, i.e. with the 'conveyance of
signals.'"[279] As regards VoIP providers, the same author argues that only those who
give access to or from the telephone network should be considered "providers of
publicly available electronic communications services".

This said, the e-privacy Directive has been amended by Directive 2009
2009/36/EC which added a provision specifically targeting the use of cookies. For
this amendment to have an impact in practice, it would make sense to include
within the category of providers of publicly available electronic communications
service providers of services supplied over the Internet.[280]

In this line, it is important to recall that providers of services over the Internet
do regularly collect personal data in the sense of the data protection Directive for
the definition to be given to that notion is quite extensive. By way of example,
while one could try to argue that those who collect IP addresses to detect copyright infringers using peer-to-peer software are not processing personal data, for as
data controllers they are not reasonably likely to use means to identify by themselves the data subjects hidden behind the IP addresses,[281] providers supplying
services over the Internet often require users to open an account with them and
thereby to communicate nominative data. Therefore, each time these providers
collect other types of data relating to their users, these additional data should be
treated as personal data as well since the service providers would be able to combine both sets of data quite easily. One could go even further and argue that the
foregoing should hold true even if it is not necessary to open any account to use
the providers' services, as long as the providers collecting different sets of data
would reasonably be able to identify with enough precision their users.[282]

Fourth, because the very distinction between traffic and non-traffic data (i.e. content
data) raises some difficulties, it is arguable that the processing imposed by the data

---

[279] Feiler at 3.

[280] See also Recital 6 of the e-privacy Directive which evokes a wide range of electronic communications services: "[t]he Internet is overturning traditional market structures by providing
a common, global infrastructure for the delivery of a wide range of electronic communications
services. Publicly available electronic communications services over the Internet open new possibilities for users but also new risks for their personal data and privacy". Notably in England,
the Court's ruling in Chambers v DPP [2012] EWHC 2157 (Admin) seems to show that the term
"public electronic communications network" must be interpreted extensively and include pri-
vately owned networks.

[281] It does not seem that the new definition of personal data to be found in the proposed general
data protection Regulation alters these findings.

[282] See the example of AOL who in 2006 published the logs of 675 000 Americans with the
intent to feed university research. The name of users had been replaced by the numbers of cookies to anonymise the logs. However, combining together all the searches corresponding to the
same numbers of cookies, some journalists managed to identify some users. More generally, see
the search facility still offered by AOL at www.aolstalker.com.

retention Directive is over-broad and thereby not necessary in a democratic society. Traffic data are deemed to cover information related to the source and destination of communications, the date, time and duration of communications, the type of communications, the types of equipment used by the communicating,[283] and are distinguished from content data or correspondences.[284] As explained by Ross Anderson taking the example of URLs, it is sometimes difficult to draw a clear line: "[p]eople might think of a URL is just the address of a page to be fetched, but a URL such as http://www.google.com/search?q=marijuana+cultivation+UK contains the terms entered into a search engine as well as the search engine's name. Clearly some policeman would like a list of everyone who submitted such an enquiry. Equally clearly, giving this sort of data to the police on a large scale would have a chilling effect on online discourse" [25]. In the UK at least, full URLs seem to be considered non-traffic data.[285]

On 8 April 2014, the CJEU thus declared the data retention Directive invalid. The Court easily characterised an interference with Articles 7 and 8 of the European Charter on fundamental rights (the right to the respect of one's private life and the right to the protection of personal data): data retention obligations imposed upon providers of publicly available electronic communications services or of public communications networks amount in themselves to a prima facie violation of the right to the respect of private life.[286]. Even more it is a particularly serious interference,[287] although the Court acknowledges that it does not adversely affects the essence of the right to respect for private life since the content of electronic communications is not retained.[288] In addition, the interference cannot be justified in this case given the paucity of the legal framework. The CJEU undertakes a strict scrutiny of the legislation.[289] It notes that the Directive covers "in a general manner, all persons and all means of electronic

---

[283] See, e.g. Article 5 of the data retention Direction and Article 2 and 6 of the e-privacy Directive 2002/58/EC.

[284] See Article 1(2) of the data retention Directive.

[285] In the UK, this issue has been heavily debated. In the end, it does seem that content data are the wining qualification. This results from a code of practice on acquisition and disclosure of communications data adopted in 2007 under Chapter II of Part I of the Regulation of Investigatory Powers Act 2000. HOME OFFICE, Acquisition and disclosure of communications data, available at http://www.homeoffice.gov.uk/publications/counter-terrorism/ripa-forms/code-of-practice-acquisition. It provides guidance on the procedures to be followed when acquisition of communications data takes place under those provisions. §2.20 reads as follow: "[i]n relation to internet communications, this means traffic data stops at the apparatus within which files or programs are stored, so that traffic data may identify a server or domain name (web site) but not a web page". However, law-makers are often less nuanced. See, for example, the statements made in the introduction to the UK Draft Communications Data Bill: "[c]ommunications data is very different from communications content—for example, the text of an email or a telephone conversation, and arrangements for the police and security agencies to intercept the content of a communication are very different from arrangements to get access to communications data".

[286] Digital Rights Ireland at [34].

[287] Digital Rights Ireland at [37].

[288] Digital Rights Ireland at [39].

[289] Digital Rights Ireland at [48].

communication as well as all traffic data without any differentiation, limitation or exception being in the light of the objective of fighting against serious crime".[290] It is not therefore a measure of targeted surveillance (the persons concerned do not have to present a link, direct or indirect with serious crime),[291] the retention is not meant to be limited to certain time periods or geographical zones in order to establish a link with a specific threat to public security,[292] no limitations are set for the access of the competent national authorities to the data and subsequent possible uses,[293] no oversight mechanisms are established,[294] the retention period is not strictly calibrated to the gravity of the threat to be prevented.[295] The data retention Directive does not also cater for the concerns of Article 8 of the Charter in the sense that there is no distinction between different types of data in relation to their degree of sensitivity, there is no guarantee that the service providers at issue will implement a high level of protection and security to retain the data, that they will retain the data within the European Union, and that the data will be destroyed at the end of the data retention period.[296] For once the connection between the protection of personal data and the right to respect for private life is strongly affirmed.[297] Remains to be seen what the implications of such a ruling will be at the national level. With this said, the upshot of the e-privacy Directive remains unchanged and it is likely that even after the recognition of the invalidity of the data retention Directive a significant amount of personal data will continue to be retained by Internet and online service providers.

To sum up, when it comes to Internet access providers and providers of services over the Internet, the leeway granted to these providers for processing personal data is quite substantial and it is not sure that the proposed general data Regulation will change this course of things. Indeed, systematic and extensive evaluation of personal aspects relating to a natural person is deemed to present specific risk only when it is done for the purpose of producing legal effects upon individuals or at least significantly affect them.[298] Besides, it is arguable whether the recognition of the invalidity of the data retention Directive will affect the leeway granted to Internet access providers and over the Internet service providers, as Fig. 1.5 tries to make it clear. This is all the more true that consent remains in many cases a mere formal safeguard and that it is only as regards special categories of processing that a faculty is offered to Member States to make consent ineffective. Nevertheless, referring back to Article 8 (as the CJEU did it) it is now clear that the systematic retention of the traffic data of all Internet users is not possible without the introduction of a long list of legal safeguards.

---

[290] Digital Rights Ireland at [57].

[291] Digital Rights Ireland at [58].

[292] Digital Rights Ireland at [59].

[293] Digital Rights Ireland at [60–61].

[294] Digital Rights Ireland at [62].

[295] Digital Rights Ireland at [64].

[296] Digital Rights Ireland at [66–68].

[297] See in particular Digital Rights Ireland at [53].

[298] See Article 33.

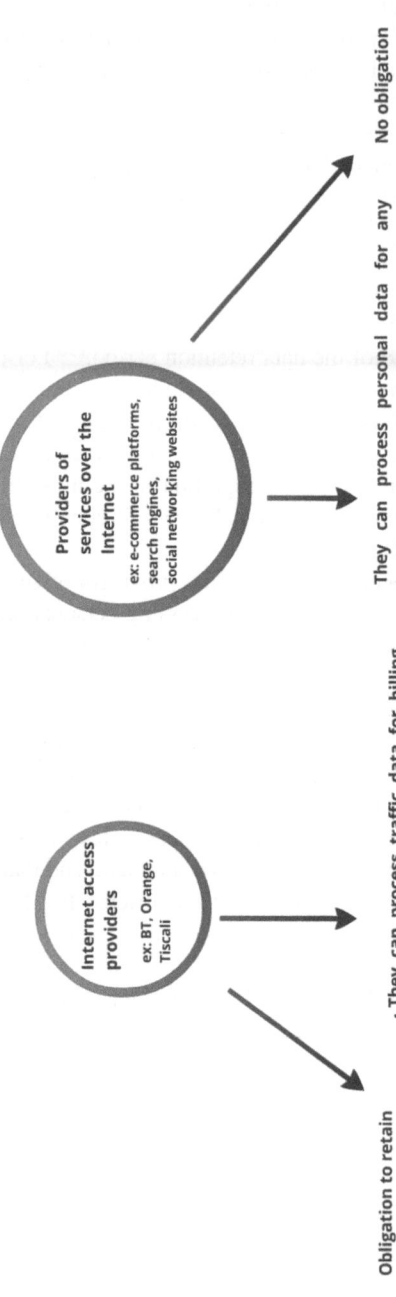

Fig. 1.5 Processing and retention of personal data by service providers

1.5 Privacy and Security

To engage in the balancing of privacy and security interests, it is crucial to start with defining the concepts at stake. The contours of the right to respect for private life have been drawn in the previous sections. What remains is to clarify the notion of security and distinguish between distinct but closely related terms such as national security, public security, the prevention of crimes and cybersecurity. Once this is done, it will become easier to understand the terms of the debate and assess the appropriateness of hot security measures such as deep packet inspection and data mining.

1.5.1 National Security, Public Security and the Prevention of Crimes

Today it is not uncommon, not to say frequent, to hear that privacy is outdated[299] and that in any case even if it had had some merit in the past, especially after the implosion of totalitarian regimes, it must today be given less weight. Indeed, the security of the society at large, as opposed to the privacy of individuals, is said to be a more urgent need given the rate at which cybercrimes are growing[300] and the seriousness of the threat of cyberterrorism.

First of all it is important to recall that both privacy and security are at the same time private and social goods and therefore benefit both individuals and the group at large. The right to the protection to one's private life is a human right in the same way as the right to the liberty and security as recognised by Article 5 of the CEDH[301] (as well as Article 6 of the European Charter of fundamental rights),[302] which states that "[e]veryone has the right to liberty and security of person. No one shall be deprived of his liberty save in the following cases and in accordance with a procedure prescribed by law". And follows a list of cases precisely described to identify safeguards necessary to protect the interests of individuals.

---

[299] See for example: Brian Wheeler, How much privacy can smartphone owners expect? (BBC News, Washington, 22 November 2011), available at http://www.bbc.co.uk/news/magazine-15730499; and Emma Barnett, Facebook's Mark Zuckerberg says privacy is no longer a "social norm" (Telegraph, 11 January 2010), available at http://www.telegraph.co.uk/technolog y/facebook/6966628/Facebooks-Mark-Zuckerberg-says-privacy-is-no-longer-a-social-norm.html. The role of privacy considering computers was even questioned in 1975, see Sol Wachtler, The right to privacy 14 Judges Journal 7, at 8 (1975).

[300] "Every second, 18 adults become a victim of cybercrime—that's more than one and a half million cybercrime victims each day globally" says the Symantec website, at http://www.symant ec.com/corporate_responsibility/topic.jsp?id=cybercrime.

[301] See also article 3 of the Universal declaration of human rights.

[302] The formulation of the European charter is a way more succinct though: "[e]veryone has the right to liberty and security of person".

By way of example, no one shall be deprived of his liberty save in the context of "the lawful arrest or detention of a person effected for the purpose of bringing him before the competent legal authority on reasonable suspicion of having committed an offence or when it is reasonably considered necessary to prevent his committing an offence or fleeing after having done so".

In addition, in as much as the security of the society is a social good, protecting the privacy interests of individuals generates positive externalities for the society as a whole. D. Solove distinguishes between the individualistic and the communitarian approaches to privacy. Building upon the view of John Dewey who argued that individual rights contribute to the welfare of the community, D. Solove explains that "the value of protecting the individual is a social one. Society involves a great deal of friction, and we are constantly clashing with each other. Part of what makes society a good place in which to live is the extent to which it allows people freedom from the intrusiveness of others. A society without privacy protection would be suffocating, and it might not be a place in which most would want to live. When protecting individual rights, we as a society decide to hold back in order to receive the benefits of creating the kinds of free zones for individuals to flourish". D. Solove is not the only voice speaking in this direction and similar remarks can be found in the work of several authors concerned about the needs of contemporary democratic societies.[303]

Having said that, the question of how to balance the values of privacy and security remains unanswered. Truly as the ECtHR stated in the Klass case "democratic societies nowadays find themselves threated by highly sophisticated forms of espionage and by terrorism, with the result that the State must be able, in order effectively to counter such threats, to undertake the secret surveillance of subversive elements operating within its jurisdiction". And the Court inferred from this consideration that it "has therefore to accept that the existence of some legislation granting powers of secret surveillance over the mail, post and telecommunications is, under exceptional conditions, necessary in a democratic society in the interests of national security and/or for the prevention of disorder or crime".[304]

However, the aforementioned formulation is slightly misleading. National security and the prevention of disorder or crime are not to be equated. Indeed, if one looks at the ECtHR's case law, it does appear that the seriousness of the offence is a very important consideration for the purpose of determining whether the interference to the right to respect for private life is justified on the ground of Article 8(2). In the words of Louise Doswald-Beck: "[t]he final decision in the S and Marper case may be compared with the Klass case in which the Court accepted the possibility of retaining material from the telephone tapping for an indefinite amount of time. The difference is that in the Klass case, there was an independent review and, more importantly, the Klass case concerned the

---

[303] See, e.g. Robert [26], Simitis [27], Cohen [28], Schwartz [29], Gavison [30], Wong [31], Oliver [32].

[304] Klass at [48].

suspicion of terrorism, whereas in the S and Marper case, the offences involved were alleged attempted robbery and harassment of partner. It is significant, therefore, that the Court stressed the severity of the offence".[305] Not to be confusing, Louise Doswald-Beck also notes that the particularly sensitive nature of the personal data collected and stored in the S and Marper case (DNA information) was also crucial to explain the ruling of the ECtHR. In the Klass case, all that was stored was the recordings of telephone conversations. That being said, taking into account all the relevant decisive parameters together, it is indeed likely "that the need for retention of personal data in terrorism cases will be given greater weight in the proportionality evaluation than for lesser offences".[306] A contrario, for lesser offences than terrorism, it should be more difficult for public authorities to justify interferences with the right to the protection of one's private life. Even more, it should not suffice to allege that public security interests are at stake to be on safe grounds. As aforementioned, the ECtHR has attempted in some cases to review the relevance of the legitimate end claimed by the public authorities even in cases in which the government alleged to act to protect national security.[307]

It is therefore inappropriate to try to oppose the values of privacy and security in general terms. Going further, it is crucial to precisely identify the type and seriousness of the security threat at stake in order to properly identify the needs of the democratic society implicated. In this line, it becomes necessary to distinguish, to the extent possible, between different, though closely related, concepts and in particular between the concepts of national security, public security and the prevention of crimes. Indeed, when "only" the prevention of crimes is at stake, it should be more difficult to justify interferences to the right to respect of private life.

With this said, the trend seems to heading towards a conflation of the terms of national security and prevention of serious crimes. In Weber, the ECtHR was fully aware that the Amendment to the German Act authorising strategic monitoring had considerably extended the range of subjects in respect of which so-called monitoring could be carried, whereas it was initially limited to armed attack on Germany.[308] Besides, it dismissed the argument of the applicant stating that "drug trafficking, counterfeiting of money and money laundering or presumed dangers arising from organised crime did not constitute a danger to public safety sufficient to justify such an intensive interference with the telecommunications of individuals".[309]

Given the lack of precision in the field, a definitional exercise is needed to show that opposing security to privacy is in many cases over-simplifying the terms of the debate.

---

[305] Doswald-Beck [33, p. 456] (Doswald-Beck).

[306] Doswald-Beck p. 456.

[307] See Segerstedt-Wiberg at [90–91]. See also Rotaru at [53].

[308] Weber at [114].

[309] Weber at [112].

Although it is difficult to find precise definitions at national level[310] with national government opting for wide-encompassing terminologies,[311] it is useful to identify three distinct concerns. The necessity to take measures to prevent terrorism acts and activities of espionage could fall within the category of national security measures. Espionage activities should be understood as activities attempting to get access to and eventually transmit and diffuse information about the national defence with intent to use that information to injure national governments.[312] As regards terrorism, it is worth mentioning the model definition to be found in a series of best practices drafted by the special rapporteur on the promotion and protection of human rights and fundamental freedoms while countering terrorism: [313]

"Terrorism means an action or attempted action where:

1. The action:
   (a) Constituted the intentional taking of hostages; or
   (b) Is intended to cause death or serious bodily injury to one or more members of the general population or segments of it; or
   (c) Involved lethal or serious physical violence against one or more members of the general population or segments of it; and

2. The action is done or attempted with the intention of:
   (a) Provoking a state of terror in the general public or a segment of it; or
   (b) Compelling a Government or international organization to do or abstain from doing something; and

---

[310] See, e.g. as regard the definition of terrorism Report of the special representative on human rights defenders, UN Doc A/58/380, 18 September 2003; Report of the Independent expert on the protection of human rights and fundamental freedoms while countering terrorism, Robert K Goldman, UN Doc E/CN.4/103, 7 February 2005; Report of the United Nations High Commissioner for Human Rights on the protection of human rights and fundamental freedoms while countering terrorism, UN Doc A/HRC/8/13, 2 June 2008; Report of the Special rapporteur on the promotion and protection of human rights and fundamental freedoms while countering terrorism, Martin Scheinin, UN Doc A/64/211, 3 August 2009.

[311] See, e.g. the website of the UK security service, the famous MI5, stating that "As a matter of Government policy, the term 'national security' is taken to refer to the security and well-being of the United Kingdom as a whole. The 'nation' in this sense is not confined to the UK as a geographical or political entity but extends to its citizens, wherever they may be, and its system of government" at https://www.mi5.gov.uk/home/about-us/what-we-do/protecting-national-security.html.

[312] The survival of the nation-state should be at stake here. See nevertheless, the words of the UK MI5 which defines espionage as "a process which involves human sources (agents) or technical means to obtain information which is not normally publically available. It may also involve seeking to influence decision makers and opinion-formers to benefit the interests of a foreign power." MI5, What is Espionage?, 2013, available at https://www.securityservice.gov.uk/home/the-threats/espionage/what-is-espionage.html.

[313] Report of the Special Rapporteur on the promotion and protection of human rights and fundamental freedoms while countering terrorism, Martin Scheinin, Ten areas of best practices in countering terrorism, 22 December 2010, UN Doc A/HRC/16/51, at [28].

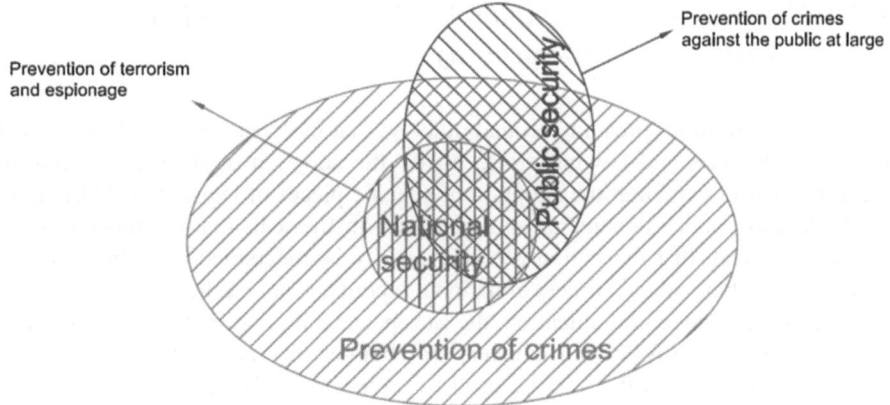

Prevention of crimes
against the public at large

Prevention of terrorism
and espionage

Fig. 1.6 Distinguishing security-related ends

3. The action corresponds to:

   (a) The definition of a serious offence in national law, enacted for the purpose
       of complying with international conventions and protocols relating to ter-
       rorism or with resolutions of the Security Council relating to terrorism; or
   (b) All elements of a serious crime defined by national law".

At the European level, two framework decisions list terrorism offences, requiring
their criminalisation, prosecution and in some cases extradition; they seem to be
more or less in line with the above definition albeit in a somewhat more detailed
and specific manner.[314]

   The category of public security measures should then be distinguished from
that of national security measures and cover measures to prevent public disorder.[315] Such measures aim at preventing criminal offences directed at the public at
large such as those relating to "disorder, health, morals" to use the terminology of
the ECHR.[316] The public safety and the economic well-being of a country could
also be included within the notion of public security for not all threats to public
security come from the commission of crimes.

   Figure 1.6 thus illustrates the interplay between the three categories of concerns. Threats to national security form the narrowest category.

---

[314] EU Council Framework Decision 2002/475/JHA on combating terrorism, 13 June 2002, OJ L
164, 22.6.2002, pp. 3–7 and EU Council Framework Decision 2008/919/JHA amending Framework
decision 2002/475/JHA on combating terrorism, 28 November 2008, OJ L 330 of 9.12.2008.

[315] Not all authors distinguish between national security and public security. See, e.g. Acquilina
[34], at 131 who adopts the following definition: "Public security as understood in this paper
encompasses a fourfold categorisation: (i) national (or state) security, (ii) public safety, (iii) the economic well-being of a country, and (iv) protection from other criminal offences directed at the public at large such as those relating to disorder, health, morals and the rights and freedoms of others".

[316] See, e.g. Article 8(2) of the ECHR.

1.5.2 National Security, Public Security, the Prevention of Crimes and Cybersecurity

Today, a new term is spreading around quickly: that of cybersecurity which is used both by politicians and law-makers to justify the adoption of sui generis security measures and in particular the adoption of specific pieces of legislation.[317] Looking at the different policy documents and legislative instruments that use this terminology it does seem that the notion of cybersecurity is understood quite broadly and easily extends beyond the borders of national security, if not public security.[318]

In its recent joint communication, the European Commission defines the term of cybersecurity in the following manner: "[c]yber-security commonly refers to the safeguards and actions that can be used to protect the cyber domain, both in the civilian and military fields, from those threats that are associated with or that may harm its interdependent networks and information infrastructure. Cyber-security strives to preserve the availability and integrity of the networks and infrastructure and the confidentiality of the information contained therein".[319] It is added that "[c]ybersecurity efforts in the EU also involve the cyberdefence dimension. To increase the resilience of the communication and information systems supporting Member States' defence and national security interests, cyberdefence capability development should concentrate on detection, response and recovery from sophisticated cyber threats".[320] The European Commission notes that threats can have different causes and in particular that threats are not necessarily linked to the commission of crimes: "Cybersecurity incidents, be it intentional or accidental, are increasing at an alarming pace and could disrupt the supply of essential services we take for granted such as water, healthcare, electricity or mobile services. Threats can have different origins—including criminal, politically motivated, terrorist or state-sponsored attacks as well as natural disasters and unintentional mistakes".[321]

In other words, cybersecurity is a large umbrella which once again covers different types of concerns ranging from the mitigation of natural disasters and unintentional mistakes to the safeguard of national security passing by the prevention of crimes.[322] It is therefore dangerous from the perspective of privacy interests to attempt to build a cybersecurity strategy without acknowledging the diversity of

---

[317] See, e.g. proposal for a Directive of the European Parliament and of the Council concerning measures to ensure a high common level of network and information security across the Union, COM (2013) 48.

[318] See, e.g. the documents listed in Rita Tehan, Cybersecurity: Authoritative Reports and Resources, April 17, 2013, available at http://www.fas.org/sgp/crs/misc/R42507.pdf.

[319] Joint communication to the European Parliament, the Council, the European Economic and Social Committee of the Regions, Cybersecurity Strategy of the European Union: An Open, Safe and Secure Cyberspace /* JOIN/2013/01 final, in fn 4 (Cybersecurity Strategy of the European Union).

[320] Cybersecurity Strategy of the European Union. See also the French White Paper Livre Blanc sur la Défense et la Sécurité nationale, Paris, Editions Odile Jacob-La Documentation Française, 2008.

[321] Cybersecurity Strategy of the European Union at [1.1].

[322] This explains why the term cybersecurity as its cousin cyberspace may be improper in as much as it seems to imply that the regulation to be applied to that space should differ in kind.

threats that are likely to emerge. This is all the more true that private actors are meant to have a leading role.[323] In its joint communication, the European Commission has indeed asked the industry to "take leadership in investing in a high level of cybersecurity and develop best practices and information sharing at sector level and with public authorities with the view of ensuring a strong and effective protection of assets and individuals, in particular through public-private partnership". Truly the difficulty with the Internet is that, although the whole network can be conceived as critical telecommunications infrastructure, it is not owned or even supervised by any public entity. It is indeed a network of many networks, many of them being private networks. It thus becomes challenging to clearly distinguish between public and private interests. Nevertheless, jeopardising the security of one particular private network should not in all cases amount to jeopardising public security or better national security as a whole; although in many instances, attacks against information systems are criminal acts.[324]

Not only is it crucial to distinguish between national security, public security and the prevention of crimes for the purpose of balancing privacy interests with security interests, but it is consequently essential not to conflate too quickly the term of cybersecurity with that of information security. The latter term is indeed used to describe the necessary attributes of ICT systems (i.e. parameters necessary to make the system secure) and is thereby meant to be neutral as regards the nature of the interests at stake, be they interests of national security, public security or criminal policies. By way of example, the International Standard Organisation defines the notion of information security as covering the "preservation of confidentiality, integrity and availability of information in the Cyberspace".[325] Article 17 of the data protection

---

[323] Interestingly, five of the biggest industrial players (Cisco Systems, IBM, Intel, Juniper Networks and Microsoft) have formed a coalition, the Industry Consortium for Advancement of Security on the Internet, to find adequate answers to security threats. See www.icasi.org.

[324] See Council Framework Decision 2005/222/JHA of 24 February 2005 on attacks against information systems OJ L 69, 16.3.2005, introducing offences such as illegal access to information systems, illegal system interference and illegal data interference and Directive 2013/40/EU of the European Parliament and of the Council of 12 August 2013 on attacks against information systems and replacing Council Framework Decision 2005/222/JHA, OJ L 218, 14.8.2013, pp. 8–14. The Directive makes illegal interception a criminal offence in order to address new modes of committing cybercrimes such as the use of botnets (networks of computer that have been infected by computer viruses).

[325] ISO/IEC 27032:2012 Information technology—Security techniques—Guidelines for cybersecurity, available at http://www.iso.org/iso/catalogue_detail?csnumber=44375. See also the definition of the International Telecommunications Union ("the collection of tools, policies, security concepts, security safeguards, guidelines, risk management approaches, actions, training, best practices, assurance and technologies that can be used to protect the cyber environment and organization and user's assets. Organization and user's assets include connected computing devices, personnel, infrastructure, applications, services, telecommunications systems, and the totality of transmitted and/or stored information in the cyber environment. Cybersecurity strives to ensure the attainment and maintenance of the security properties of the organization and user's assets against relevant security risks in the cyber environment. The general security objectives comprise the following: availability; integrity, which may include authenticity and non-repudiation; and confidentiality") in ITU—Recommendation X.1205 (04/2008) available here: http://www.itu.int/rec/T-REC-X.1205-200804-I.

Directive can be seen as a means to ensure information security. It requires the implementation of security measures to prevent "accidental or unlawful destruction or accidental loss, alteration, unauthorised disclosure or access" of/to personal data.

All in all, the European Commission lost the occasion to clarify and hierarchize the list of regulatory objectives to be pursued at the European level: network and information security, cybercrime and defence. This is all the more problematic that each element of the cybersecurity strategy is to be administered by a different body and in particular ENISA and EUROPOL within which we now find EC3.[326] At a national level it is not clear to which extent data protection authorities and CERTs' roles overlap.

1.5.3 Balancing Privacy and Security

Once the concepts are clarified, it becomes easier to understand that the "nothing to hide" argument which has been used in particular by government officials in order to justify a low level of privacy protection and legitimise surveillance techniques is both misleading and distorting. The nothing to hide argument is usually expressed in the form of the following slogan: "if you have nothing to hide, you have nothing to fear". Yet, such an argument relies upon a series of controversial assumptions.[327]

The first one is that "[p]rivacy involves a person's 'right to conceal discreditable facts about himself'".[328] As it should now be clear after the foregoing description of the ECtHR's case law and data protection principles, such a conception is a way too narrow.

The second one is that security interests always completely override privacy interests.[329] Not all security measures are intended to prevent the same type of threats. Terrorism is far from being a frequent threat.[330] In any case, even if national security interests are at stake, this does not mean that review and mitigation mechanisms are not legitimate. In other words, safeguards as regards the type and amount of data collected and stored, the duration of the storage, the recognition of data subject rights such as a right to erasure, a right to access or a right of notification, and safeguards to make sure the personal data collected can only be

---

[326] [35]

[327] In this line see Solove [36] (Solove, Nothing to hide).

[328] Solove, Nothing to hide, at 751. D Solove quotes the words of Richard Posner in Richard A. Posner, Economic Analysis of Law 46 (5th ed. 1998).

[329] Solove, Nothing to hide at 753.

[330] See e.g. BBC, Terror attacks levelled out, says 10-year study 4 December 2012, available at http://www.bbc.co.uk/news/world-20588238; and "On the one hand, terrorism is relatively infrequent and hard to predict; on the other hand, when it starts to happen there is a tendency for it to happen in the same place a lot". The Institute for Economics and Peace Global Terrorism Index: Capturing the Impact of Terrorism for the Last Decade (2012), available at http://www.visionofh umanity.org/wp-content/uploads/2012/12/2012-Global-Terrorism-Index-Report1.pdf.

used and shared for specific purposes, can in most cases be put in place without jeopardising the effectiveness of security measures.

Even more, guaranteeing the security of individuals requires in many instances the implementation of effective privacy measures. This is particularly true in cyberspace for one of the major threats is that of identity theft.

A recent report of the European Commission meant to examine EU citizen's experience and perceptions of cybersecurity issues,[331] looked at Internet users' experience of and concerns about different types of cybercrimes. It found that "[a] round a third of internet users across the EU (32%) say they have received an email or phone call fraudulently asking for access to their computer, logins or personal details. This is by far the most common type of cybercrime experienced by respondents. In total, 7% of internet users say that this has happened to them often, while 25% say it has happened occasionally". In this report, identity theft is described as the act of stealing personal data and impersonating the data subject, e.g. shopping under one's name. In reality, sending emails to fraudulently ask for personal details, i.e. phishing,[332] is one of the many ways identity thefts are committed, which thus confirms that fraudulent impersonation is a major concern in cyberspace, be it the result of personal data theft or not.[333] Going further, the expression "identity theft" as such is misleading as the person victim of such an act does not end up being deprived of her identity. Identity thefts is a form of fraud or deceit which is not always characterised as a crime.[334]

Angus Marshal and Brian Tompsett, offering an overview of the scene as it was in 2005, highlight the variety of the techniques used to fraudulently impersonate individual or company identities.[335] Among the list of methods mentioned, one can find:

---

[331] Special Eurobarometer 404, November 2013, Report on Cyber-security, survey conducted by TNS Opinion and Social, available at http://ec.europa.eu/public_opinion/archives/ebs/ebs_404_en.pdf. In the USA, in 2007 at least, identity theft seemed to be the most common online fraud: "[t]he United States Federal Trade Commission has labelled identity theft as the most common type of consumer fraud, affecting thousands of people every day. In fact, approximately 40 % of the frauds reported to the United States Federal Trade Commission (2007) over the last few years has involved some type of identity theft". Chad Albrecht, Conan Albrecht and Shay Tzafrir, How to protect and minimize consumer risk to identity theft 18 Journal of Financial Crime 405, at 405 (2011).

[332] Generally understood as a "form of online identity theft that aims to steal sensitive information from users such as online banking passwords and credit card information. Phishing attacks use a combination of social engineering and technical spoofing techniques to persuade users into giving away sensitive information (e.g. using a web form on a spoofed web page) that the attacker can then use to make a financial profit." Kirda and Kruegel [37], at 554.

[333] The aforementioned definition of identity theft is too narrow for it does not include a more recent trend relying upon acquisition of data voluntarily released by data subjects.

[334] This is the case in England. See Oxford v Moss (1979) 68 Cr. App. R. 183 in fine. The Computer Misuse Act of 1990 is indeed of limited use here.

[335] Marshal and Tompsett [38] (Marshal and Tompsett). For a broader approach to the issue of identity theft not merely focusing upon online identity theft, see, e.g. Albrecht et al. [39].

- Protocol weakness[336]
- Naïve users[337]
- Malicious software[338]

In the end given the variety of identity theft technique and the growing threat posed by aggregation of data easily accessible, the authors deplore the use of email addresses as a frequent authentication token.[339]

The importance of data acquisition techniques used to misrepresent the identity of individual at a second stage shows that not only is it necessary to secure confidential information but also it is crucial to minimise the amount of personal data voluntarily released by Internet users,[340] hence the importance of the data minimisation principle.

While the protection of privacy interests is crucial to reduce the frequency of cybercrimes, this has not always been fully acknowledged by policy and law-makers, as the story of the regulation of cryptography[341] shows it. Mads Anderson and Peter Landrock wrote in 1996 that "the only way to protect the integrity, authenticity, non-repudiation and confidentiality of data communication, is by using cryptographic functions".[342] However, obviously "law enforcement and perhaps essential parts of government intelligence activities may be obstructed".[343] As a result "the need for businesses and individuals to secure communication by encryption and the need for governments to be able to intercept communication has created a confrontation between two valid interests"[344] which has had consequences upon both the way the legal framework has been designed and implemented and the technology has evolved.

The call for "trusted" third parties was the direct consequence of such a confrontation. Escrow schemes were advocated to make users escrow their keys to "trusted" third parties who could be required to hand over these same keys to

---

[336] Marshal and Tompsett at 131.

[337] Marshal and Tompsett at 132.

[338] Marshal and Tompsett at 132–133.

[339] Marshal and Tompsett at 129.

[340] Data acquisition should constitute a fraud punished by criminal sanctions in the same way as the use of email scams or malicious software. Under s.2 of the UK Fraud Act of 2006 a fraud by misrepresentation is committed when a person "(a) dishonestly makes a false representation, and (b) intends, by making the representation [either] (i) to make a gain for himself or another, or (ii) to cause loss to another or to expose another to a risk of loss". However, contrary to the use of phishing techniques, it is only when the personal data are used that a misrepresentation will occur, hence the importance of data protection rules. See on the legal implication of phishing techniques Savirimuthu and Savirimuthu [40].

[341] Understood in modern times as a synonym of encryption, which involves the transformation of intelligible information into unintelligible information.

[342] Anderson and Landrock [41], at 342 (1996) (Anderson and Landrock).

[343] Anderson and Landrock at 342.

[344] Anderson and Landrock at 342. For an overview of the debate at the end of the 1990s see e.g. Anderson and Landrock [41], Gerard and Broze [42], Ward [43], Akdeniz and Walker [44], Sundt [45], Bert-Jaap Koops [46], Kennedy et al. [47].

law-enforcement bodies under certain conditions.[345] Yet, resorting to "trusted" third parties was to be accompanied by an increasing risk of data theft.

After much debate, key disclosure laws have been preferred. They have been adopted to force individuals to surrender keys to law-enforcement bodies as Chapter III of RIPA 2000 illustrates it.[346]Other Member States have also followed a similar approach to gaining access to encrypted materials.[347] This explains why at the international level, the Council of Europe's Cybercrime Convention[348] requires that signatories "adopt such legislative and other measures as may be necessary to empower its competent authorities to order any person who has knowledge about the functioning of the computer system or measures applied to protect the computer data therein to provide, as is reasonable, the necessary information"[349] "to empower its competent authorities to search or similarly access: (a) computer system or part of it and computer data stored therein; and (b) a computer-data storage medium in which computer data may be stored in its territory".[350] However, key disclosure laws have also been criticised for being over-broad and allowing access to personal information that may not be relevant to the crime under investigation, as well as violating the privilege against self-incrimination.[351]

---

[345] See, e.g. in the UK, the proposal of the Department of Trade and Industry to set up a key escrow system in DTI, Licencing of Trusted Third Parties for the Provision of Encryption Services, March 1997, available at http://www.fipr.org/polarch/ttp.html. For a critique of these techniques, see Hal Abelson, Ross Anderson, Steven M. Bellovin, Josh Benaloh, Matt Blaze, Whitfield Diffie, John Gilmore, Peter G. Neumann, Ronald L. Rivest, Jeffrey I. Schiller, Bruce Schneier, The Risks of Key Recovery, Key Escrow, and Trusted Third-Party Encryption, 1997, available at http://www.schneier.com/paper-key-escrow.pdf.

[346] Part III of the RIPA did not enter into force until 2007. S.49(2) of chapter III ensures that so long as "any person with the appropriate permissions under schedule 2" has reasonable grounds to believe:

(a)   "that a key to the protected information is in the possession of any person,
(b)   that the imposition of a disclosure requirement in respect of the protected information is—
   i.   necessary on grounds falling within subsection (3), or
   ii. necessary for the purpose of securing the effective exercise or proper performance by any public authority of any statutory power or statutory duty,
(c)   that the imposition of such a requirement is proportionate to what is sought to be achieved by its imposition, and
(d)   that it is not reasonably practicable for the person with the appropriate permission to obtain possession of the protected information in an intelligible form without the giving of a notice under this section",

They may impose a "disclosure requirement in respect of the protected information" by notice to the person "whom he believes to have possession of the key".The necessary grounds mentioned in s.49(3) comprise the protection of the interests of national security, the prevention or detection of crime and the pursuit of the interests of the economic well-being of the United Kingdom.

[347] For example, The Netherlands, France and Belgium.

[348] The Convention (ETS 185). At the time of writing, 42 States are Parties to the Convention and 11 States have signed it.

[349] Article 19(4).

[350] Article 19(1).

[351] See in the UK, the case R v S(F) and A(S) [2008] EWCA Crim 2177.

As the example of identity theft shows it, information security attributes such as confidentiality, availability, integrity, authenticity are thus key to make the number of fraudulent and deceptive behaviour decrease. Yet these attributes also participate to ensuring a high degree of privacy. At the same time, the will to develop monitoring capacities on the part of policy makers but also businesses result in increasing the probabilities of misuse of personal information. A strict Article 8 scrutiny of surveillance measures, be they implemented by public or private actors, is thus crucial.

1.5.4 Scrutinising Surveillance Measures

Although data mining techniques and deep packet inspections can serve several purposes, they are becoming full-fledged instruments of surveillance used both by private actors and governments with a view of instilling more security within the network or society itself. However, it is arguable whether all the practices relying upon the use of such techniques[352] comply with data protection law and privacy law in general, in particular if they are used as tools of mass surveillance against all users in a systematic manner outside of any accessible and foreseeable framework. Even more, it is arguable that in some cases, these practices really contribute to increasing security. First, they increase the level of monitoring and thereby the probability of misuses of personal information. Second, when followed by sanctions these practices simultaneously increase the risk for individuals of being treated unfairly without being able to understand the reasons for the decision taken.[353] Being unable to understand the reasons for decisions affecting oneself inevitably feeds a feeling of insecurity.

1.5.4.1 Deep Packet Inspection[354]

The use of deep packet inspection techniques in the shadow of the law bears witness to the fact that security interests tend to be "grossly" weighted against privacy interests.

Deep packet inspection allows Internet service providers to screen computer network packets and depending upon the degree of intrusion chosen examine both packet headers and packet payload as packets pass through a check point. Passing through a check point to inspect the different layers of a packet can mean in

---

[352] It is important to distinguish between the technology itself and the way the technology is used in order to assess its legitimacy.

[353] Solove, Nothing to hide at 756. D. Solove uses the metaphor developed in Franz Kafka's novel The Trial to explain that at least two distinct concerns are at stake because of the use of surveillance techniques: the inhibition or chilling of individuals' behaviour and the frustration of individuals being unable to understand the reasons for the decisions affecting their interests. They are thus in a state of "helplessness and powerlessness". See also Solove [48].

[354] For a deeper analysis of the legal scrutiny deployed to confine deep packet inspection practices, see Stalla-Bourdillon et al. [49].

practice that the packet will be diverted to follow another route and eventually pass by a proxy server.[355] It is important to recall though that in principle, the routing of packets over the network only require the inspection of IP headers (i.e. the inspection of the IP address of the destination of the packets).

In practice, it is difficult to determine the extent to which deep packet inspection is used for there is not full transparency on the matter. This said, this technique has been used and is used for targeted advertising and traffic management and network security purposes.[356] Contrary to other forms of tracking methods, such as cookies, deep packet inspection is more invasive in the sense that it allows Internet service providers to obtain a very comprehensive knowledge of their subscribers' habits and tastes: as all data outgoing from a subscriber's computer are inspected, Internet service providers can potentially inspect all searches through the means of search engines, all web pages browsed, and all emails sent.

What is important to bear in mind at this stage is that it is very likely that all the data collected by Internet service providers end up being qualified as personal data for the purposes of data protection law since in most cases, unless effective anonymising measures are implemented, they should be able to identify the person behind the data collected by resorting to reasonable means and, e.g. by matching different data sets.[357]

The seriousness of the interference with the right to respect for private life depends upon the type of communication, (i.e. whether the communication is ultimately intended to reach the public at large or a limited section of the public) and the degree of intrusion of the inspection (whether the inspection is aimed at identifying the headers of the packet, the IP header or the TCP header, or whether it is

---

[355] See, e.g. the way the Cleanfeed technology functions as explained in Richard Clayton, Anonymity and traceability in cyberspace, 2005, Technical Report, pp. 120–121, available at http://www.cl.cam.ac.uk/techreports/UCAM-CL-TR-653.html.

[356] See the development of an updated version of Einstein intrusion-detection programme (Einstein 3), which relies upon deep packet inspection of the ".gov" traffic, to detect attacks and malware, especially associated with e-mail. The aim is to "not only be able to detect malicious traffic targeting Federal Government networks, but also prevent malicious traffic from harming those networks. This will be accomplished through delivering intrusion prevention capabilities as a Managed Security Service provided by Internet Service Providers (ISP). Under the direction of DHS [Department of Homeland Security], ISPs will administer intrusion prevention and threat-based decision-making on network traffic entering and leaving participating federal civilian Executive Branch agency networks", http://www.dhs.gov/privacy-documents-national-protection-and-programs-directorate-nppd. See, however, the privacy impact assessment conducted for Einstein 3 available at http://www.dhs.gov/sites/default/files/publications/privacy/PIAs/PIA%20NPPD%20E3A%2020130419%20FINAL%20signed.pdf.

[357] See Recital 26 of the data protection Directive. See also the Article 29 Working Party (1/2008 (WP148) p. 8 ("An individual's search history is personal data if the individual to which it relates, is identifiable. Though IP addresses in most cases are not directly identifiable by search engines, identification can be achieved by a third party. Internet access providers hold IP address data. Law enforcement and national security authorities can gain access to these data and in some Member States private parties have gained access also through civil litigation. Thus, in most cases—including cases with dynamic IP address allocation—the necessary data will be available to identify the user(s) of the IP address").

also aimed at identifying the content of the payload and in particular the URL of a search string or the very content of an email). It is not clear, however, which elements of the payload fall within the legal category of content of communication.

One difficulty stems from the question whether deep packet inspection amounts to an interception of communication in the same way as telephone wiretapping. As long as the service provider has not received the consent of both the person who has sent the communication and the intended recipient of the communication, (when it is not the public at large obviously), and the interception is not necessary for the purpose of transmitting the communication itself, deep packet inspection could amount to an unlawful interception if it targets the content of confidential communication. Indeed, deep packet inspection takes place when the data are in transit. Interestingly, this remains contentious. Truly as the distinction between communication content and traffic data is difficult to draw, it could be argued that depending upon its degree of intrusiveness deep packet inspection does not always amount to an interception of a communication understood as communication content. This said, the ECtHR's definition of correspondence is quite broad and does seem to include traffic data such as the numbers dialled for they allow identifying the recipients of communications.[358]

If however one follows the words of Charleton J., an Irish Judge who had to hear a copyright dispute between right holders and an Internet service provider, deep packet inspection does not seem to ever amount to an interception of communication. Deep packet inspection, he said, "is not the seeking of information which is in the course of transmission. Instead, it identifies the nature of transmissions, whether encrypted or otherwise, by reference to the ports which they use, and the protocol employed, as to identify peer-to-peer communication. UPC [the Internet service provider] does this already for legitimate commercial purposes related to the management of transmissions. If it suited, they could also easily identify the file # of copyright works and block them or divert the search in aid of theft to a legal site. This is not a general search for information. It is simple use of deep packet inspection technology in aid of proper transmission".[359]

Even if the qualification of interception is not retained for the interference has been committed for a purpose connected with the provision of a telecommunications service, i.e. traffic management narrowly defined,[360] or because the data is not in transit, or because no confidential communication is at stake, this does not mean that the processing becomes automatically lawful.

---

[358] see supra pp. 22 ff

[359] EMI Records (Ireland) Ltd and Others v UPC Communications Ireland Ltd, [2010] IEHC 377, §107. The Copysense technology was at stake in this case.

[360] See, for example, the wording of RIPA 2000 which provides in its Sect. 3(2) that "(3) Conduct consisting in the interception of a communication is authorised by this section if—

(a) it takes place for purposes connected with the provision or operation of that service or with the enforcement, in relation to that service, of any enactment relating to the use of postal services or telecommunications services".

Truly, it is not enough to pursue a legitimate end in order to make the processing lawful. The processing must also be of quality and secure and thereby be undertaken in compliance with the data quality and data security principles found in the data protection Directive. In particular, the data collected shall be adequate, relevant and not excessive in relation to the purposes for which they are collected and/or further stored or used. Besides, the data shall be kept in a form which permits identification of data subjects for no longer than is necessary for the purposes for which the data are processed. Importantly, to be able to assess whether the principle of finality (or purpose limitation) and of limited duration are complied with, it is necessary to understand the more precise reason lying behind the constraint of traffic management or security of the network.

Assuming the technique of deep packet inspection is used as a measure of surveillance to systematically and/or permanently collect and store information relating to the private life of individuals which includes information publicly accessible (in this case, private information equates personal data in the sense of data protection law)[361] Article 8(2) scrutiny should step in. The use of such a technique should therefore only be justified if the norms governing its implementation are accessible and clearly stated and more precisely if the norms governing the selection, storage, sharing, access, and destruction of the information are clearly stated to prevent abuses. Consent in itself should not be enough to make the measure of mass surveillance lawful.

In this regard, the intended use of the collected data is an important factor to take into account to determine whether the interference is proportionate to the end pursued and thereby necessary in a democratic society. Where sanctions and in particular technological sanctions, such as the termination of an account, or the slowing down of the communication speed, the impossibility to access a website or use a particular application, or even quarantining, follow the deep packet inspection, the interference should be more difficult to justify.

Although not very often mentioned, Article 15 of the data protection Directive is of relevance here for it provides that "[m]ember States shall grant the right to every person not to be subject to a decision which produces legal effects concerning him or significantly affects him and which is based solely on automated processing of data intended to evaluate certain personal aspects relating to him, such as his performance at work, creditworthiness, reliability, conduct, etc".[362] Therefore, when deep packet inspection is not only used as a monitoring technique but also as a preliminary step for the subsequent sanctioning of users' behaviour, it necessarily becomes more suspicious.

---

[361] If deep packet inspection is used to safeguard the security of the network, it is in fact likely to be used as a measure of surveillance.

[362] The vagueness of Article 15(2) which is aimed at carving exceptions to Article 15(1) could mean that in practice the right not to be subjected to a decision based solely on automated processing is a mere formal protection.

	"Mere" traffic data	Content data
1	In principle the collection and storage of traffic data should not amount to an interception of communication. Note however that the ECtHR seems to adopt a broad definition of correspondence including the number dialled.	Whether the interference amount to an interception of a confidential communication.
2	What is the purpose of the collect?Is it a legitimizing end? Has consent been given?	
3	Is the processing done in compliance with the data quality and data security principles?	
4	Are the norms governing the selection, storage, sharing, access, and destruction of information clearly stated and accessible?	
5	Is the processing proportionate to the end pursued? Note that consent should not always justify the processing.	

Fig. 1.7 Scrutinising uses of deep packet inspection

To sum up, in order to assess the lawfulness of deep packet inspection used as a surveillance measure targeting personal data, one should try to identify the type of data at stake and answer the questions listed in Fig. 1.7 in context.

The use of Phorm's technology by certain Internet service providers[363] illustrates the challenge posed by deep packet inspection technologies. Phorm's Webwise system is said not to store IP addresses. However, it relies upon the processing of the content of web pages visited, search terms and URLs combined with advertising categories in order to send to Internet users relevant advertising[364] (contextual marketing). Even if Internet service providers using this technology are not storing the IP addresses of Internet users for the purposes of tracking their behaviour down, these providers are likely to be still processing personal data given the variety and richness of the datasets collected and stored, and the technological means at their disposal allowing them to combine these datasets together and/or eventually with subscribers data.

Assuming both Internet users and website operators have not given their consent, Internet service providers implementing Phorm's Webmise system could be deemed as intercepting confidential communications if the terms of the transactions are meant to remain confidential. Besides, even if consent has been expressly given by both Internet users and website operators, Internet service providers still have to comply with data quality and data security principles. What is more, even if they comply with these principles, remains the argument that are still missing appropriate legal safeguards for regulating access to the data collected and stored, the security of their retention, and their eventual destruction.

Truly, the issue of the lawfulness of deep packet inspection techniques is further complicated by the imposition of an obligation, upon Internet service

---

[363] Phorm has had several Internet access providers for partners and in particular the UK service providers BT, TalkTalk and Virgin media. Public outcry at the national level followed by the condemnation of the EU Commission has managed to convince UK Internet service providers to stop implementing this technology. Outside the UK, Phorm has been dealing with Oi, Telefonica in Brazil, TTNET-Türk Telekom in Turkey, and Romtelecom in Romania.

[364] See the website of the company for a description of the technology used, available at http://www.phorm.com/technologies.

providers, to use such techniques in order to prevent their subscribers from accessing copyright infringing websites. However, to take an example, Arnold J. while ordering, in the UK Newzbin2 case,[365] the defendant (the Internet service provider BT) to expand its use of the Cleanfeed technology and implement it to block access to the infringing website Newzbin2, he did not even address the privacy implications of the use of the deep packet inspection technology at stake. Indeed, it was implicit in his findings that deep packet inspection techniques, when used to collect IP addresses of websites and URLs, on a systematic basis against all subscribers without any limit of duration, was necessary in the democratic society for it had to be implemented to defend the rights of others, the copyright owners. Nothing was said about the need to state clear norms in relation to the selection, storage, sharing, access and destruction of the personal data collected.

This is slightly neglecting Article 8. Yet if the use of the technology at stake implies the systematic or permanent retention of traffic data, Article 8 scrutiny is warranted. It goes without saying that when law-enforcement agencies implement themselves deep packet inspection technologies, as the Tempora scandal illustrates it,[366] Article 8(2) scrutiny is still relevant.

1.5.4.2 Data Mining

Deep packet inspection is one way out of many to obtain personal data. Collected personal data can then be organised in datasets and eventually matched up with other datasets. Automated profiling is the next step, which from the perspective of privacy protection, creates problem of its own as hinted above. Individuals progressively lose control over themselves for they begin to be affected by decisions solely based on an automated process without understanding the reasons for such decisions, without being able to participate to the decision-making process and ultimately without being able to react upon these decisions to defend their rights.

Although the negative consequences of profiling have been condemned for quite some time and by many,[367] it is still unclear what the legal status of such a technique is in particular when they do not rely upon the implementation of intrusive techniques such as deep packet inspection.

Data mining has been defined as the "nontrivial extraction of implicit, previously unknown, and potentially useful information from data".[368] What must be clear is that the data mined do not need to be confidential. Said otherwise unknown information should be understood as implicit information for the data mined once again can be publicly available. That the data mined are publicly

---

[365] Twentieth Century Fox Film Corp v BT [2011] EWHC 1981 (Ch).

[366] See supra p. 4 and pp. 54–55.

[367] See e.g. Marx [50], Lyon [51], Hildebrandt and Gutwirth [52], Koutsias [53], Schermer [54] (Schermer). See also Fulda [55], Tien [56], Kawakami and McCarty [57], Slobogin [58], Rubinstein et al. [59], Solove [60].

[368] Schermer, at 45 citing Frawley et al. [61, p. 58].

available does not mean that data mining is innocuous from the perspective of the
protection of privacy interests. At least two modalities of data mining techniques
can be identified depending upon the aim pursued by the data miner:

- Descriptive data mining or unsupervised data mining: "[t]he goal of descriptive
  data mining is to discover unknown relations between different data objects in a
  database….By discovering correlations between data objects in a dataset that is
  representative of a certain domain, we can gain insight to it".[369]
- Predictive data mining or supervised data mining: "the goal of predictive data
  mining is to make a prediction about event based on patterns that were determined using known information".[370]

That being said, whatever the purpose pursued, data mining amount to processing
of personal data each time an individual can be identified directly or indirectly as a
result of the use of such a technique.[371]

Nothing says in the data protection Directive that the collection, storage or use
of publicly available information is excluded from the scope of the data protection
Directive. The only thing that is mentioned is that the processing of sensitive data
cannot be prohibited when the information is publicly available.[372] As a result, even
though the processing cannot be prohibited in principle, it should still pursue a
legitimate end, be of quality and be secure. In other words, it should still be undertaken in compliance with data quality and data security principles and in particular
with the principle of finality (or purpose limitation). This thus means that depending upon its modalities, its scope, its duration and its effect upon individuals, the
processing could still be ultimately condemned.

Once again, when the processing is intended to impact upon the situation of
individuals, it is more suspicious, as acknowledged by Article 15 of the data protection Directive which constraints Member States to grant individuals a right not
to be subject to decisions based solely on automated processing of data.

This being said, despite the merits of European data protection law, it is doubtful
whether it is able to effectively frame the development of data mining techniques for
at least two reasons. First the legal framework seems to be more ambiguous at second
glance. Article 10 of the proposed general data Regulation reads as follows: "[i]f the
data processed by a controller do not permit the controller to identify a natural

---

[369] Schermer, at 45.

[370] Schermer, at 45.

[371] As aforementioned, the means at the disposal of the data controller must be taken into
account to determine whether the person is identifiable.

[372] See Article 8 which provides namely that "1. Member States shall prohibit the processing
of personal data revealing racial or ethnic origin, political opinions, religious or philosophi-
cal beliefs, trade-union membership, and the processing of data concerning health or sex life.
2. Paragraph 1 shall not apply where:… (e) the processing relates to data which are manifestly
made public by the data subject or is necessary for the establishment, exercise or defence of legal
claims". The same exclusion is to be found in the proposed general data protection Regulation.
See Article 9(e).

person, the controller shall not be obliged to acquire additional information in order to identify the data subject for the sole purpose of complying with any provision of this Regulation".[373] Depending upon one's understanding of the term acquire, an a contrario reading of this provision would have the consequence that when the data controller has access to different data sets at no additional cost he would be obliged to use data mining techniques in order to identify the data subjects concerned and "empower" them by making sure they are well informed and dispose of several other guarantees such as the right to rectification or the right to be forgotten and erasure.

Second, even though one agrees that in principle, European data protection law is not indifferent to data mining activities and could be used to restrain their diffusion by enforcing data quality and data security principles, it is unlikely that these safeguards will act as real brakes.

In this line, even if the proposed general data protection Regulation is adopted, data protected impact assessment seem to be unsurprisingly one-sided. When examining processing presenting specific risks to the rights and freedoms of data subjects, the data controller will "simply" be asked under Article 33 to "address the risks, safeguards, security measures and mechanisms to ensure the protection of personal data and to demonstrate compliance with [the] Regulation, taking into account the rights and legitimate interests of data subjects and other persons concerned". The data controller will not be asked to demonstrate that the processing is a key component of an effective security measure the results of which could not be obtained by least costly alternatives. In other words, no strict scrutiny of the security measure relying upon the processing of personal data will be undertaken.

As the ECtHR's case law shows it, the systematic collection and storage of information publicly accessible amounts to a prima facie interference with the right to the protection of private life when used as measures of surveillance.[374] They thus should be justified. In other words, a normative framework should confine the use of such a practice by setting clear norms in relation to selection, storage, sharing, access and destruction of the information. Besides, the proportionality of the measures to the end pursued should be assessed by taking into account the degree of seriousness of the offence and/or anti-social behaviour to be prevented and the nature of the information collected.

Article 8 of the ECHR is thus crucial here, for application of its paragraph 2 offers the possibility of scrutinising the appropriateness of measures of surveillance and in particular data mining activities on the ground of a proportionality test and of expressly posing the question whether the measures at stake will be effective or whether less costly alternatives do exist.

In this regard, it is interesting to note that there is no consensus upon the usefulness of data mining techniques for the purpose of preventing crimes in general and more serious crimes such as terrorism. Bruce Schneier compares credit card

---

[373] For a similar view, see [62].

[374] It is interesting to note that in the USA, the fourth Amendment protection does not seem to apply to data mining unless it amounts to a search. See e.g. Tien [56], Kawakami and McCarty [57], Slobogin [63].

fraud with terrorism and explains that obviously terrorist plots are different from credit card fraud plots:

"Many credit-card thieves share a pattern—purchase expensive luxury goods, purchase things that can be easily fenced, etc.—and data mining systems can minimise the losses in many cases by shutting down the card. In addition, the cost of false alarms is only a phone call to the cardholder asking him to verify a couple of purchases. The cardholders don't even resent these phone calls—as long as they're infrequent—so the cost is just a few minutes of operator time.

Terrorist plots are different. There is no well-defined profile and attacks are very rare. Taken together, these facts mean that data-mining systems won't uncover any terrorist plots until they are very accurate, and that even very accurate systems will be so flooded with false alarms that they will be useless".[375]

B. Schneier adds that this is the rarity of the threat when it comes to terrorism that makes the tracking system useless for the probability of encountering a false positive[376] or a false negative[377] significantly increases in that situation.[378]

The recent attempt in the UK to pass the Draft Communications Data Bill[379] shows that the need to adopt a strict scrutiny approach to assess surveillance measures before their implementation is not widely shared. The Bill aimed at ensuring the availability of communications data[380] stored by telecommunications operators.[381] Communications data are defined very broadly, which could have meant that

---

[375] Bruce Schneier [64] (Schneier, Data Mining).

[376] "A false positive is when the system identifies a terrorist plot that really isn't one". Schneier, Data Mining.

[377] "A false negative is when the system misses an actual terrorist plot". Schneier, Data Mining.

[378] Schneier, Data Mining.

[379] Presented to Parliament by the Secretary of State for the Home Department by Command of Her Majesty I June 2012 Cm 8359 Available at http://www.parliament.uk/draft-communications-bill.

[380] Under clause 28 communications data comprise subscriber data ("information...held or obtained by a person providing a telecommunications service about those to whom the service is provided by that person"), use data ("information about the use made by a person of a telecommunications service or in connection with the provision to or use by any person of a telecommunications service") and traffic data ("data which is comprised in, attached to or logically associated with a communication (whether by the sender or otherwise) for the purposes of a telecommunication system by means of which the communication is being or may be transmitted...").

[381] Not only Internet access providers seemed to be concerned but also over the Internet service providers for providers of services merely facilitating the use of telecommunications systems are also targeted. See clause 28, which defines telecommunications operators in the following manner: "a person who (a) controls or provides a telecommunication system, or (b) provides a telecommunications service". A telecommunication system is "a system (including the apparatus comprised in it) that exists (whether wholly or partly in the United Kingdom or elsewhere) for the purpose of facilitating the transmission of communications by any means involving the use of electrical or electro-magnetic energy". And a telecommunication service is a "service that consists in the provision of access to, and of facilities for making use of, a telecommunication system (whether or not one provided by the person providing the service)".

telecommunications operators would have had to retain data that would have been irrelevant for their businesses purposes.[382] A wide range of information would thus have been collected and thereby accessible by public authorities which would have been given the possibility to put through one data request for several telecommunications operators.[383] The justification for such a piece of legislation was found in numbers. Presently about 25 % of communications data required by investigators is unavailable and without intervention this will increase to 35 % within 2 years stated the Home Office.[384] The intention of the drafter is thus to bring availability back to around 85 % by 2018.[385] However, the numbers put forward have not generated consensus. The Joint Committee of the House of the Lords and the House of Commons was quite sceptical as its reports show: "[w]e are of the strong view that the 25 % data gap is an unhelpful and potentially misleading figure. There has not been a 25 % degradation in the overall quantity of communications data available; in fact quite the opposite. Technological advances and mass uptake of Internet services since RIPA was passed in 2000, including social networking sites, means that there has been, and will continue to be, a huge increase in the overall amount of communications data which is generated and is potentially available to public authorities".[386] The Draft Communications Data Bill should, however, be buried for quite some time after Snowden's revelations and the death of the data retention Directive.[387]

---

[382] Clause 1 is very generic in terms: "[t]he Secretary of State may by order (a) ensure that communications data is available to be obtained from telecommunications operators by relevant public authorities in accordance with Part 2, or (b) otherwise facilitate the availability of communications data to be so obtained from telecommunications operators". The Home Office stated in the Explanatory Notes to the draft Bill that in practice that would mean that telecommunications operators would be required to generate all "necessary" communications data for the services or systems they provide; to retain "necessary" communications data, and even to process the data to ease the efficient and effective obtaining of the data by public authorities. Data mining techniques could thus be imposed upon such providers. There is, however, no indication as to what "necessary" communications data means. Joint Committee of the House of Lords and House of Commons, Report on the Draft Communications Data, December 2012, available at http://www.parliament.uk/draft-communications-bill/, p. 23.

[383] Clause 14 provides a power to establish filtering arrangements to make it easier for public authorities to acquire communications data. Public authorities would be able to submit one request through the Request Filter which would then interrogate the databases of several telecommunications operators and automatically selecting the data to supply public authorities with "only" the relevant data. Joint Committee of the House of Lords and House of Commons, Report on the Draft Communications Data, December 2012, available at http://www.parliament.uk/draft-communications-bill/, p. 34.

[384] Home Office written evidence, paragraphs 13 and 15.

[385] Home Office written evidence, paragraph 16.

[386] Joint Committee of the House of Lords and House of Commons, Report on the Draft Communications Data, December 2012, available at http://www.parliament.uk/draft-communications-bill/, p. 16.

[387] See BBC, Nick Clegg: No "web snooping" bill while Lib Dems in government 25 April 2013, available at http://www.bbc.co.uk/news/uk-politics-22292474. See nonetheless BBC, Fresh proposals' planned over cyber-monitoring 8 May 2013, available at http://www.bbc.co.uk/news/uk-politics-22449209.

1.6 Conclusion

To conclude, it should be clear by now that the values of privacy and security cannot simply be conceived as being in blunt opposition without any possibility of reconciliation. In fact, it is likely that in the end, these values should be conceived as complementary rather than contradictory. Indeed, the (European) right to respect for private life (to be preferred to the notion of right to privacy) has seen its material scope to extend over the years to cover both secret and public activities. The "raison d'être" of the protection of private life is to be found in the protection of human dignity implying securing the personal autonomy of individuals and their abilities to relate with others. In other words, both the liberty of private life and the secrecy of private life are legally protected. Therefore, the systematic collection and storage of publicly accessible information as much as the collection and storage of information relating to physical identity of individuals or the interception and/or the monitoring of confidential communications amount to prima facie interferences with the right to respect of private life protected by Article 8 of ECHR. While such measures of surveillance can end up being legitimate, they have to be justified and thereby scrutinised, as the ECtHR's case law shows it. This is to make sure a satisfactory normative framework is in place clarifying the instances in which information pertaining to the private life of individuals can be collected, stored, shared, accessed, destroyed, and the use of the information at stake is proportionate to the end pursued.

It is true that another set of rules has been developed alongside Article 8 of the ECHR partly to ease the free flow of information, i.e. the free flow of personal data among Member States. This being said, European Union data protection law should not be viewed as undermining the logic of Article 8. It complements Article 8 more than supplants it. This is the case in particular when persona data are systematically collected and stored or permanently stored. In such a case, the category of private information and personal data overlap.

Necessarily rougher than Article 8 and in particular Article 8(2) case law for it has been elaborated as a proactive regulatory instrument, data protection law was first of all intended to serve as daily guidance for data controllers at a time at which the concept of private life was maturing. But a familiar skeleton emerges from the analysis of common and sectorial rules of data protection law: the necessity to purse legitimate ends, the urge to implement safeguards such as users' rights to ensure the transparency, quality and security of the processing, and the insistence upon the proportionality of the processing. With this said, the assessment of the proportionality of the processing for the purposes of applying data protection law remains partial for the broader picture cannot be considered. No precise standards are set within the legislation or its implementation measures to clarify the procedures to be followed for selecting, storing, sharing and accessing or destructing relevant personal data. Indeed, the data protection Directive is a horizontal instrument. In addition, the proportionality of the whole security strategy relying upon the processing of personal data (whether it will indeed contribute to increase the overall level of security within society and whether less costly alternatives exist) is not a relevant consideration to determine whether the processing is lawful. Besides, the multiplication of data retention obligations has certainly weakened data protection principles.

As a result, data protection law has to be combined with a robust interpretation of Article 8 of ECHR, which should mean that more detailed rules have to be formulated in each sector. Besides, in several instances, if not in many, the pressing need to guarantee security should require a high level of privacy protection and thereby to minimise the collection, secure the storage, prevent some forms of sharing and eventually inform data subjects.

What remains unsettled is how broad is the range of surveillance measures that fall within the domain of Article 8 and should be subject to scrutiny. As practices and technologies evolve, it is difficult to give a clear-cut answer.

Despite definitional uncertainties, the foregoing could appear a rather optimistic description of the state and potentiality of European privacy law broadly defined. Enforcement of European privacy law is a big issue though, which makes it difficult to predict whether we are in fact not done yet. There is another related issue that could not be covered in the framework of this chapter but which should be in the minds of all European law-makers and citizens. Ensuring a high level of privacy and security within the European Union is not enough to adequately protect European citizens since the advent of cloud computing. When personal data are transferred to non-European jurisdictions, there is no legal mechanism that ensures that the law enforcement and intelligence gathering agencies of these non-European jurisdictions will not have easily access to these data. Hence the crucial need to develop a robust cloud computing industry in Europe.[388]

Obviously, it is challenging to keep pace with the advancement of the technology and make sense of a normative framework in an ever changing technological environment. But the will to promote and use innovation should not at the same time blind policy makers and law enforcers.

Acknowledgments I would like to thank Callum Beamish for his excellent research assistance and Michéal O'Floinn and Ed Bates for fruitful discussions. All mistakes are mines.

References

1. Lyon, D. (2003). *Surveillance after September 11*. Cambridge: Polity Press.
2. Seamon, R., Gardner, W. (2004). The Patriot Act and the wall between foreign intelligence and law enforcement. *Harvard Journal of Law & Public Policy, 28*, 319.
3. Schulhofer, S. (2006). The new world of foreign intelligence surveillance. *Stanford Law & Policy Review, 17*, 531.
4. The Draft Communications Data Bill (2012, June). Cm 8359, available at http://www.official-documents.gov.uk/document/cm83/8359/8359.pdf. Accessed 7 May 2013.
5. Bruce Schneier (2013). The Internet is a surveillance state, March 16, 2013, available at http://edition.cnn.com/2013/03/16/opinion/schneier-internet-surveillance.

---

[388] see Fighting cyber crime.

6. Rigaux François, M. (1980). La liberté de la vie privée. Revue internationale de droit comparé. *Juillet-septembre, 43*(3), 539–563.
7. Warren, D., Brandeis, L. (1890/1891). The right to privacy. *Harvard Law Review, 4,* 193.
8. Richards, N., & Solove, D. (2007). Privacy other's path: recovering the law of privacy. *Georgetown Law Journal, 96,* 123.
9. Whitman, J. (2004). The two western cultures of privacy: dignity versus liberty. *The Yale Law Journal, 113,* 1151.
10. Prosser, W. (1971). *The law of torts* (4th ed.). St. Paul: West Publishing Company.
11. Prosser, W., et al. (1984). *Prosser and Keeton on torts* (5th ed.). Stavanger: West Group.
12. Solove, D. J. (2006). A taxonomy of privacy. *University of Pennsylvania Law Review, 154,* 477.
13. Kayser, P. (2005). Protection de la vie privée, Economica, Paris, n 8.
14. Sweet, A. S., Keller, H. (2008). The reception of the ECHR in national legal orders. Faculty Scholarship Series, Paper 89, available at http://digitalcommons.law.yale.edu/cgi/viewcontent. cgi?article=1088&context=fss_papers.
15. Sweet, A. S., Keller, H. (2008). Assessing the impact of the ECHR on national legal systems, Paper 88, available at http://digitalcommons.law.yale.edu/cgi/viewcontent.cgi?article=1087 &context=fss_papers.
16. Moreham, N. A. (2008). The right to respect for private life in the European convention on human rights: a re-examination. *European Human Rights Law Review, 44*(1), 19.
17. Solove, D. (2002). Conceptualizing privacy. *California Law Review, 90,* 1087.
18. Solove, D. (2006). *The digital person: technology and privacy in the information age.* New York: New York University Press.
19. Costa, L., & Poullet, Y. (2012). Privacy and the regulation of 2012. *Computer Law & Security Review, 28,* 254.
20. Robinson, N. et al. (2009). (RAND) Review of the European data protection directive (2009 RAND), available at http://www.rand.org/content/dam/rand/pubs/technical_reports/2009/ RAND_TR710.pdf.
21. Pearce, G., & Platten, N. (1998). Achieving personal data protection in the European Union. *Journal of Common Market Studies, 36,* 529–547.
22. Mayer-Schönberger, V. (1998). Generational development of data protection in Europe. In P. E. Agre & M. Rotenberg (Eds.), *Technology and privacy: the new landscape* (pp. 219–229). Cambridge: The MIT Press.
23. Reidenberg, J. R. (1992). The privacy obstacle course: hurdling barriers to transnational financial services. *Fordham Law Review, 60,* S137.
24. Feiler, L. (2010). The legality of the data retention directive in light of the fundamental rights to privacy and data protection. *European Journal of Law and Technology, 1*(3), 1.
25. Anderson, R. (2008). *Security engineering* (2nd ed., p. 782). New York: Wiley.
26. Robert, C. (1989). Post, the social foundations of privacy: community and self in the common law tort. *California Law Review, 77,* 957.
27. Simitis, S. (1987). Reviewing privacy in an information society. *University of Pennsylvania Law Review, 135,* 707–709.
28. Cohen, J. E. (2000). Examined lives: informational privacy and the subject as object. *Stanford Law & Policy Review, 52,* 1373–1438.
29. Schwartz, P. M. (1999). Privacy and democracy in cyberspace. *Vanderbilt Law Review, 52,* 1609–1613.
30. Gavison, R. (1980). Privacy and the limits of law. *The Yale Law Journal, 89,* 421.
31. Wong, S. (1996). The concept, value and right of privacy. *UCL Jurisprudential Review, 3,* 165.
32. Oliver, H. (2002). Email and internet monitoring in the workplace: information privacy and contracting-out. *Industrial Law Journal, 31*(4), 321.
33. Doswald-Beck, L. (2011). *Human rights in times of conflict and terrorism* (p. 456). Oxford: Oxford University Press.
34. Acquilina, K. (2010). Public security versus privacy in technology law: a balancing act? *Computer Law & Security Review, 26*(2), 140.

35. Bigo, D. Boulet, G. Bowden, C. et al., (2012). *Fighting cyber crime and protecting privacy in the cloud.* Study 2012 for the Directorate-General for Internet Policies, p.22 (Fighting cyber crime)
36. Solove, D. (2007). I've got nothing to hide" and other misunderstanding of privacy. *San Diego Law Review, 44,* 745.
37. Kirda, E., & Kruegel, C. (2006). Protecting users against phishing attacks. *The Computer Journal, 49*(5), 554.
38. Marshal, A., & Tompsett, B. (2005). Identity theft in an online world. *Computer Law & Security Report, 21,* 128.
39. Albrecht, C., Albrecht, C., & Tzafrir, S. (2011). How to protect and minimize consumer risk to identity theft. *Journal of Financial Crime, 18,* 405.
40. Savirimuthu, A., & Savirimuthu, J. (2007). Identity theft and systems theory: the fraud act 2006 in perspective. *SCRIPTed—A Journal of Law, Technology & Society, 4*(4), 437.
41. Anderson, M., Landrock, P. (1996) Encryption and Interception. *Computer Law and Security Report 12,* 342.
42. Gerard, P., & Broze, G. (1997). Encryption: an overview of European policies: I.T., telecoms and broadcasting. *Computer and Telecommunications Law Review, 3*(4), 168.
43. Ward, C. (1997). Regulation of the use of cryptography and cryptographic systems in the United Kingdom: the policy and practice. *Computer and Telecommunications Law Review,3,* 105.
44. Akdeniz, Y., & Walker, C. (1998). UK Government policy on encryption: trust is the key? *Journal of Civil Liberties, 3,* 110.
45. Sundt, C. (1999). Law enforcement and cryptography: a personal view. *Computer and Telecommunications Law Review* 187.
46. Koops, B.-J. (1996). A survey of cryptography laws and regulations. *Computer Law and Security Report, 12,* 349.
47. Kennedy, G. (2000). Codemakers, codebreakers and rulemakers: dilemmas in current encryption policies. *Computer Law and Security Report, 16*(4), 240.
48. Solove, D. (2004). *The digital person: technology and privacy in the information age* (p. 47). New York: New York University Press.
49. Stalla-Bourdillon, S., Papadaki, E., Chown, T. From porn to cybersecurity passing by copyright: how mass surveillance techniques are gaining legitimacy (forthcoming).
50. Marx, G. T. (1985). The surveillance society: the threat of 1984-style techniques. *In the Futurist, 19,* 21–26.
51. Lyon, D. (2003). *Surveillance as social sorting, privacy risk and digital discrimination.* New York: Routledge.
52. Hildebrandt, M., & Gutwirth, S. (2008). *Profiling the European citizen.* New York: Springer.
53. Koutsias, M. (2012). Privacy and data protection in an information society: how reconciled are the English with the European Union privacy norms? *Computer and Telecommunications Law Review,18,* 261.
54. Schermer, B. W. (2011). The limits of privacy in automated profiling and data mining. *Computer Law and Security Review, 27,* 45.
55. Fulda, J. (2000/2001). Data mining and privacy. *Albany Law Journal of Science & Technology, 11,* 105.
56. Tien, L. (2004). Privacy, technology and data mining. *Ohio Northern University Law Review, 30,* 389.
57. Kawakami, S., & McCarty, S. (2004–2005). Privacy year in review: privacy impact assessments, airline passenger pre-screening, and government data mining. *I/S: A Journal of Law and Policy, 1,* 219.
58. Slobogin, C. (2008). Government data mining and the fourth amendment. *University of Chicago Law Review 75,* 317.
59. Rubinstein, I. S., Lee, R. D., & Schwartz, P. M. (2008). Data mining and internet profiling: emerging regulatory and technological approaches. *The University of Chicago Law Review, 75,* 261.

60. Solove, D. (2008). Data mining and the security-liberty debate. *The University of Chicago Law Review, 74*, 343.
61. Frawley, W.J., Piatetsky-Shapiro, G., Matheus, C. J. (1992). Knowledge discovery in databases: an overview in AAI Magazine, Fall, p. 58.
62. Winton, A., Cohen, N., (2012). *The general data protection regulation as it applies to online advertising, e-commerce and social media 18 computer and telecommunications Law 97*, p. 98.
63. Slobogin, C. (2008). Government data mining and the fourth amendment. *The University of Chicago Law Review, 75*, 317.
64. Bruce, S. (2006). Why data mining won't stop terror, 2006 commentary available at http://www.wired.com/politics/security/commentary/securitymatters/2006/03/70357.

Chapter 2
A Future for Privacy

Joshua Philips and Mark D. Ryan

Abstract We discuss how the personal privacy that we are used to as a way of life is continuously being threatened by modern technology. We divide these threats into different categories based on who the perpetrator is, and the extent to which the privacy invasion was intended by the system designer. We discuss in detail how some technologies, like the web, compromise privacy. We explain why privacy is important and describe the conflict between privacy and law enforcement. Finally, we explain our ideas for the future, which include a system for verifiable accountability to allow citizens to see what and how much information is collected and used. We give some examples of how such technology could be used in the future.

2.1 Introduction: Privacy Concerns

Internet companies such as Google and Facebook are collecting data about you and assembling profiles of you to serve the most effective advertisements. Cars are tracked across the country using number-plate recognition cameras. The transmissions from your smart electricity metre could let burglars know when you are out. We are already letting privacy take a back seat as we head at full speed into the information age.

The privacy invasions we have today will get far worse, as technology permeates our lives over the coming decades. Perhaps in the future, it will be routine to point a mobile computer at someone and, using cloud-based face recognition and database search, thereby see that the target person is single, likes cats and Italian restaurants, and that you met him once before at a homeopathy clinic in east London. Maybe you will also find out that he was prosecuted for tax evasion 12 years ago, from the millions of historical news articles that are searched almost instantly. Maybe we will interact with computers through wireless neural taps implanted in our brains and powered by glucose from the bloodstream. They had read our thoughts directly from our brains and send them wirelessly to the

© The Author(s) 2014   91
S. Stalla-Bourdillon et al., *Privacy vs. Security*, SpringerBriefs in Cybersecurity,
DOI 10.1007/978-1-4471-6530-9_2

computer, so that we could send e-mail and surf the web without using interfaces such as keyboards. The implants would be provided free of charge, as long as we agree that our thoughts will be monitored and analysed to deliver the most relevant adverts yet.

If computers become such an intimate part of our lives, technologies to preserve privacy online would need to become as normal as curtains over a window to maintain the level of personal privacy that we are used to.

How close is this sort of augmented reality scenario? Not that close. Current brain interfaces are nowhere near capable of reading thoughts; the best we have achieved is controlling computer cursors and robotic arms [1, 48]. In contrast, facial recognition is already in use. In June 2011, Facebook introduced "tag suggestions", a feature that uses facial recognition software to automatically identify people in uploaded photographs. Even though this is restricted to friends and cannot be used to identify strangers, many users were uncomfortable with this new feature [4]. In the same year, it was demonstrated that one out of ten pseudonymous user profiles could be matched with Facebook profiles using publicly available photographs. A second experiment, using a restricted data set by taking photographs of students in a college campus and finding their Facebook profiles, matched about one third of participants, using an average of less than 3 s of computation time per person [10].

2.1.1 The Problem

Information technology is inherently privacy invasive, because generally its usefulness can be improved by collecting and analysing per-individual usage records. The big internet companies today, such as Google and Facebook, are pioneers of this sort of data analysis, and use it aggressively to improve their service in a variety of ways [27]. On top of this, governments and law enforcement agencies use information technology to track and monitor the behaviour of citizens, and their communication [6]. As more and more of our behaviour and communication involves information technology, the effectiveness of this kind of monitoring increases.

But privacy appears to be a core human need. Throughout history, humans at all levels of society have sought to maintain secrets. People need to keep secrets, in order to maintain purposeful relationships with others. For example, to maintain her credibility as a professional, a dentist prefers to keep secret from her patients and colleagues the details of illnesses she may have, the nature and frequency of her sexual fantasies, her financial profile, and the conversations she has with her partner. If these were disclosed to her colleagues and patients, it would change their attitude towards her in a way she would not like. People might jump to incorrect conclusions, if the data they access is erroneous or incomplete. They may try to blackmail her, or, more mundanely, merely spam her, based on their impression of her vulnerabilities. In summary, it seems that humans want to have privacy in order to avoid:

- the consequences of incorrect conclusions that result from deliberate or accidental errors in the data, or misinterpretations, or prejudice;
- blackmail or extortion, or other abuse of power, by people with access to data; and
- commercial and other kinds of pestering (e.g. spam)

For these reasons, the right to privacy is enshrined in the European Convention on Human Rights; its Article 8 accords the citizen the "right to respect for his private and family life, his home and his correspondence". Similar foundational legislation exists in the USA. The fourth amendment to the US Constitution provides the "right of the people to be secure in their persons, houses, papers, and effects, against unreasonable searches and seizures". In the UK, privacy from data collection and processing by business organisations is supported by the Data Protection Act 1998. Edward Snowden (who at the time of writing this chapter has temporary political asylum in Russia) identifies two reasons for objecting to the mass-surveillance that he has revealed as taking place. The first is the chilling effect, namely, that people moderate their behaviour when they know that they are being watched. "Under observation, we act less free, which means we effectively are less free" [7]. The second objection arises because of retrospective investigations that mass-surveillance allows. Because the data is collected about everyone, a permanent record of everyone's daily lives is made, whether they are suspects or not. Whenever someone becomes a target for investigation at some time, the government has a very complete record of them, potentially for the whole of their life so far. "You might not remember where you went to dinner on 12 June 2009, but the government does" [7].

The problem this chapter addresses is therefore: how can privacy be maintained, in the face of the immense pressures for data collection that appear to be inevitable consequences of information technology? There are no simple answers, but we hope to describe some possibilities that could, with further research, lead to answers in some situations. The question is not just about technology; it also involves sociology, psychology and law. We intend to focus on the ways in which technology can help, though we recognise the need for contributions from those other fields.

2.1.2 Overview of Chapter

The following sections categorise privacy threats to help understand their different effects and different requirements for defending against them; then we describe ways technologies like e-mail and the web can be used to collect information about—and build profiles of—users, and we discuss various means to mitigate it. Finally, we discuss our vision for the future and describe some opportunities to develop and use privacy-friendly technology.

Table 2.1 Taxonomy of privacy threats, with some examples

Threat from	Designed	Opportunistic
Big brother Governments	Governments accessing transport, communication and financial databases, with democratic mandate	Governments introducing backdoors or deliberate vulnerabilities into cryptography implementations; governments imposing fake SSL certificates
Middle brother Corporations	Companies exploiting data obtained through usage of their services, such as Yahoo Mail, Google Drive, Facebook	Companies spying on people's behaviour through protocol or implementation vulnerabilities or spyware. Examples include the Facebook "like" button
Little brother Individuals	Inadvertent disclosures by misunderstanding social networking application privacy settings (such as those of Facebook). Neighbours, friends and strangers pointing at people cameras or Google Glass with automatic face recognition and lookup	Neighbours, friends and strangers using exploits of vulnerabilities present in e-passports and mobile phone protocols, in order to track physical presence of other people

Big, middle and little brothers are three kinds of agents that threaten our privacy. "Designed" means that the privacy threat is present by the design of the system in question; "opportunistic" means that the threat was not intended or anticipated by the designers

2.2 Taxonomy of Privacy Threats

Table 2.1 is a classification of privacy threats by who causes the threat. The threat can come from *big brother* (governments), *middle brother* (corporations) or *little brother* (individuals). Our taxonomy also distinguishes between data collection that is above-board and designed to be there, and data collection using unintended opportunities, often based on attacks that exploit software vulnerabilities. It is important to decide which of these categories to defend against. This classification helps to think clearly about the different effects of each, and the different approaches and countermeasures they may require.

2.2.1 Big Brother (Governments)

Named after the elusive yet seemingly all-seeing character from George Orwell's dystopian novel *Nineteen Eighty-Four*, our *big brother* category covers surveillance by governments, police forces and intelligence organisations.

In the past, government spying required a dedicated detective, which was expensive, so surveillance could practically only be used in a targeted way, on suspects during an investigation. Now that computers are everywhere, surveillance of millions of people, most of whom are not suspected of crimes, is easily carried out. We give a few examples to illustrate our taxonomy.

Designed: Governments have introduced technologies that allow them to carry out surveillance of their citizens. The UK police force tracks vehicles around the country using thousands of automatic number-plate recognition cameras [44] and keeps a database of political activists and journalists [45]. In 2008, MI5 asked for access to London Transport's Oyster card database, which contains information about more than 34 million travel cards [35, 53]. The UK's Communications Capabilities Development Programme is a mass internet and telephony surveillance scheme [26, 50, 52].

Government agencies of other countries also conduct secret mass-surveillance. The USA National Security Agency monitors domestic and international internet traffic [59] and continues to expand [12, 42].

Since mass-surveillance on the internet can be hindered by using encryption, there have been attempts to regulate its use. Concerns about using encryption to prevent surveillance began to arise in the 1990s in the USA. "The same encryption technology that can help Americans protect business secrets and personal privacy can also be used by terrorists, drug dealers and other criminals [36]". To solve this, in 1993, the National Security Agency in the USA tried to introduce a key escrow device, called the "clipper chip", to provide "secure telecommunications without compromising the ability of law enforcement agencies to carry out legally authorised wire-taps", [36]. When a clipper chip makes an encrypted datagram, it also produces another data item called the "Law Enforcement Access Field" (LEAF) which encodes the encryption key [14]. Since the intended recipient can decrypt the datagram only if it possesses the LEAF as well as the decryption key, the sender is obliged to send the LEAF along with the datagram. Intelligence agencies can collect the datagram and the LEAF by traditional wire-tapping means. Because they possess a global key, they can decrypt the LEAF and thereby extract the datagram decryption key. Because of opposition by academics and lack of incentives for industry to take up the clipper chip, the device did not catch on.

Opportunistic: At the time of writing this chapter, the Edward Snowden revelations have revealed the extent to which governments have been acting covertly and without democratic mandate to collect masses of data about internet users [8]. The National Security Agency (NSA) of the USA has since 2007 run a program called PRISM which forces the major internet companies to hand over e-mail and other content of their users [6]. Moreover, to keep this mass-surveillance covert, those companies have had to publicly deny such activity [41].

In a more sinister step, the NSA and the UK GCHQ have forced vendors of encryption hardware and software to cripple their implementations, for example by generating weak keys, or by inserting "back doors" that can be exploited by the security agencies [55]; again, those companies are ordered not to reveal their involvement in this subversion. In other cases, the FBI and the German government have also used spying software installed on people's computers without their knowledge [3, 5, 56, 65].

2.2.2 Middle Brother (Corporations)

We use *middle brother* to refer to companies gathering all sorts of information about their customers. Some examples:

Designed: Free computing services such as Google Mail and Facebook collect information about their user customers to use for advertising and market research, in exchange for the free service. In this ubiquitous business model, it may be more accurate to think of the advertisers as the real customers of the service provider, and the users as their product. Companies are able to build sophisticated profiles of their users, based on the content of messages that the users send and receive, and can directly exploit those profiles for marketing or other purposes, or sell them to others that exploit them (for example, reference agencies, home mortgage providers and insurance companies).

Even companies that do not require users to log in can obtain this kind of data. Many internet protocols have mechanisms to identify users over long sessions. Although this is desirable in many cases, it can be abused. Advertisers can use mechanisms designed for tracking users, such as cookies (see Sect. 2.3.2.1), to collect information about users.

Opportunistic: Additionally to the ways of tracking users which are parts of the design of web protocols, companies can opportunistically use unintentional protocol properties to collect information about users. The Facebook "like" button is an example. It allows Facebook to track the web pages that a user visits, irrespective of whether the user clicks the button or not (see Sect. 2.3.2.1).

Mobile phone protocols also accidentally provide opportunities for tracking customers as they move around a shop. The company *Path Intelligence* does exactly this, claiming a precision of "a few metres" [47]. Information about how customers walk around shops, and perhaps between shops, is very valuable to businesses, yet could be considered private.

Public awareness of software called *iQ Agent* installed on millions of mobile telephones by mobile service providers came about after Trevor Eckhart published a report about its capabilities in 2011 [25]. Sold by *CarrierIQ*, it can report battery usage, what applications are being used and for how long, text message and voice call activity, the user's input ("screen touch events"), and information about HTTP connections [19].

In 2005, Sony BMG started including anti-copying software on some of their music CDs. The software was set to run automatically when the CD was inserted into a computer running Windows or Mac OS and would report what album titles and artists' targets were listening to as well as interfering with their ability to copy music [30]. Sony BMG's software also included serious security vulnerabilities that were exploitable by web pages [2].

2.2.3 Little Brother (Individual People)

We refer to the hypothetical nosy person who might like to find out a little more about their friends, family or neighbours as *little brother*. Examples:

Designed: Sometimes, social network websites have complicated privacy settings, and information someone uploads about themself might end up being public by mistake. Even without mistakes like this, some people do not think about the consequences of publishing information about themselves and upload information that is interesting to their employer, potential employer or colleagues. Thirteen employees for an airline lost their jobs after commenting about passengers on Facebook [58]. Tax collectors also find some of this information useful for finding tax evaders and faults [61]. Burglars can use social sites to discover when a house will be empty [18], suggesting a lack of awareness about how easy it is to search for this kind of information.

Another kind of example concerns tagging: social network sites allow users to upload content (such as photos, locations or posts) about other users. Thus, information about you posted by others is linked to your profile, which you might not like.

Camera-enabled mobile phones (and their reincarnation as wearable glasses) mean that real-time information about formerly private situations (like meetings, parties, train journeys, restaurant dinners) may be routinely uploaded and made publicly available and correlated with other information. When combined with cloud-based facial recognition, this could enable situations where, when looking around you, the people you see are accompanied by brief biographies, superimposed by your glasses.

Opportunistic: As well as using products and services created for the purpose, little brother can exploit bugs and vulnerabilities in systems which may even have been designed to prevent privacy abuses. For example, it is possible, with only a $50 RFID reader, to identify a passport's RFID chip [20] and thus track the physical location of someone's passport. The range at which RFID tags can be read is somewhat limited, so this is not very effective. A more effective way for an individual person to track someone is by their mobile telephone, using a device called an *IMSI catcher*, which can work at a distance of hundreds of metres. An *international mobile subscriber identity* (IMSI) is the identity string of a telephone SIM card, and thus of a telephone user. The mobile phone designers specifically wanted to prevent unauthorised wireless signal readers from being able to read the IMSI, and therefore they created temporary identifiers, called TMSIs, which would change frequently. Unfortunately, the design of the protocols, including 2G, 3G and 4G, is flawed, and various attacks are possible permitting individuals to check IMSIs and thus track the presence of other phones (see [11] and the references therein).

2.3 Perception and Examples

2.3.1 Current Perceptions

Observing what people from huge computing companies have to say suggests a future with very little privacy. Pointing out that some areas of modern life already lack privacy, Larry Ellison, the chief executive officer of Oracle Corporation, gives some examples. "Well, this privacy you are concerned about is largely an illusion. All you have to give up is your illusions, not any of your privacy. Right now, you can go onto the internet and get a credit report about your neighbour and find out where your neighbour works, how much they earn and whether they had a late mortgage payment and tons of other information" [13]. Eric Schmidt, former CEO of Google Inc., has similar thoughts. "We do not need you to type at all. We know where you are. We know where you have been. We can more or less know what you are thinking about [54]". Former marketing director of Facebook, Randi Zuckerberg, said "anonymity on the internet has to go away" in order to reduce bullying on the internet. "People behave a lot better when they have their real names down. I think people hide behind anonymity and they feel like they can say whatever they want behind closed doors [17]". Yet Bruce Schneier, cryptographer and computer security specialist, said that "mandating universal identity and attribution is the wrong goal". He says that anonymity "would not work", and explains that "universal identification is impossible" because of technical challenges and jurisdictional problems, and will "only give criminals and hackers new ways to hide" [62].

2.3.2 Examples

Everything we do that involves computers is a threat to our privacy, because the computers record our actions. As our lives become lived ever more online, this threat is increasing. In this section, we delve into a few of the mechanisms that have evolved to explain some of the complexities and to work out what can be done to avoid the privacy invasions.

2.3.2.1 The Web

The original idea of the web in 1991 was simply that users could fetch static pages held on servers, and view them. But it quickly became apparent that it would be useful if the traffic could go in both directions: users might type information into forms, and the pages they get back could be dynamically generated based on the user's input. To get this interaction going, the server needs to have some understanding of what state the user's browser is in, for example, whether it has visited a page before. This mechanism is provided in several ways; the best known one is the *cookie*. A cookie is a small piece of data initially given by a server to a browser. Later, when the browser interacts again with the server, the browser sends the cookie back. The server can update the cookie, and thereby track the browser's activity. Twenty years later and after two US Federal Trade Commission hearings into their privacy implications, cookies are now an integral part of the World Wide Web and are used for managing a website's state, authenticating to a website and by advertising companies for tracking users.

Terms such as "web 2.0" and "software as a service" are used to describe how the web is now used for multiway communication, document editing and publishing, and so on, and is now the main way we find things on the internet. The more we use the web as a pervasive substitute for activities previously done by other means, the more important privacy becomes. With over half the population of Europe and over three quarters of the USA using the internet [33], it has become more important than ever.

Deep packet inspection: The simplest way to spy on a web user is to look at what is sent over the network between the user and the web server. This is called *deep packet inspection*, and internet service providers (ISPs) are in a good position to do this. Deep packet inspection takes internet protocol (IP) frames and analyses the higher layer protocols—in this case, HTTP—to see visited URLs, page content, uploaded files and submitted text. An ISP can collect this information without the user or the web server being able to find out.

The web advertising business organisation Phorm created *Webwise*, a targeted advertising system that uses deep packet inspection and alteration. A user's requests are modified by Phorm's equipment at the user's ISP. Cookies are forged and redirections are inserted [21]. The redirections are to a webwise.net server, to set a tracking cookie for the webwise.net domain. By impersonating the server that the user wanted to connect to, the same tracking cookie is also set for other domains that the user visits, thus circumventing the same-origin policy of HTTP cookies and establishing a cookie that is sent to all websites. With deep packet inspection, the cookie can then be extracted from every HTTP request and the *Webwise* system can track the user everywhere. As the former chief operating officer of Phorm said, *Webwise* "actually can see the entire internet [64]". This activity is classified as "middle brother" and "opportunistic". With government snooping such as for the Communications Data Bill, ISPs have to collect data on behalf of the government, which would also be a considered a "big brother" ("opportunistic") privacy violation.

"Little brother" can also do the same in some circumstances. With the right software, anyone can intercept traffic in unencrypted wireless networks—in hotels, for example—or intercept traffic in an open wireless network that they control, and have encouraged others to connect to. No special hardware is needed to intercept traffic and acquire someone's session cookies. A Firefox add-on called *Firesheep* was released in 2010 to make it very easy [31]. The add-on listens to wireless network traffic and displays a list of intercepted user accounts for a selection of websites.

The HTTP link between the browser and the server can be encrypted, using a protocol called transport layer security (TLS). When used properly, the resulting combination (known as HTTPS) protects against deep packet inspection. However, it is possible to circumvent TLS, especially if the user can be tricked. To be secure, TLS needs a way to verify that a certain cryptographic key belongs to the server it is supposed to, instead belonging to an attacker such as a rogue ISP. TLS is normally used with a "certificate authority": an organisation that certifies the key ownership. A weakness is that any certificate authority can issue certificates for any domain names. For example, CA DigiNotar's compromise in 2011 led to an attacker obtaining a certificate valid for Google's domain names [51], even though Google had nothing to do with DigiNotar. So, a malicious or hacked certificate authority might incorrectly issue certificates, thus compromising the encryption and allowing a privacy invasion.

Even when working properly, TLS only protects the content of the HTTP stream, which includes the web page itself, content submitted by the user, and the path, query string and fragment identifier parts of URLs. TLS cannot hide the domain names that the user is visiting. That requires an anonymity network such as Tor (see Sect. 2.3.3).

Cookies: introduced at the start of this section, are specified as an extension to HTTP 1.1 in RFC 2109 (and again in RFC 6265) and are supported by almost all web browsers and servers. Having been designed for tracking, there are mechanisms for controlling how they are used.

Web servers can tell browsers how long to store cookies for, with the max-age and expires attributes, and can set which domain a cookie is for. For example, complaints.example.com might tell visitors to send their session identifier cookies to all example.com domains.

Advertisers and data mining sites such as Facebook use cookies to collect information about users. As a violation of privacy, cookies and cookie substitutes fall into the "middle brother" and "designed" categories.

Most web browsers allow their users to choose which domains to return cookies to, and in the extreme case, can return no cookies at all. This would prevent some websites from working but would completely prevent tracking by cookies. Most browsers can also list the cookies, showing their origins and contents.

However, HTTP has some features that, although not designed for tracking, can be used for such. In fact, any feature that requires the browser to store and retrieve information has potential to be used for tracking.

Caching: Most websites have resources that rarely change: logos, style sheets and so on. It would be wasteful to transfer these repeatedly, each time a browser needed them. HTTP provides mechanisms for caching resources so that a browser can store copies of them for use again later. This presents a problem: caching is a way for the browser to store something, and retrieve it again later—a bit like cookies. It is not too surprising, then, that it can be used for tracking. To set such a "cookie", the server can send a unique version of a JavaScript script, say `tracking.js`, containing a new identifier for the user. To retrieve the "cookie" again, some JavaScript code on the page just needs to load `tracking.js`, extract the unique identifier and send it to the server. This tracking can be defeated by refusing to run JavaScript.

In normal operation, a web browser needs to determine whether a resource has been updated since it cached a copy of it. HTTP provides two ways of doing this:

- The server sends a time stamp with each resource, in the `Last-Modified` header. For future requests, the browser can send an `If-Modified-Since` header with the same time stamp, and the server will only send the full response if the resource has been modified after that time.
- The server sends an *entity tag* with each resource, in the `ETag` header. The entity tag represents the current version of the resource, and is typically a hash of the

entity data. For future requests, the browser can send an `If-None-Match` header with the same tag value, and the server will only send the full response if the tag for that resource has changed.

The server only needs to choose a unique identifier for a new user and encode it in the entity tag or time stamp. Then, the next time a user requests the same resource, their browser will send the encoded identifier back to the server. Note that JavaScript is not required at all.

This can be averted with time stamps if the browser adds or subtracts a small random offset to or from the times it receives. This does not work with entity tags, so the `If-None-Match` header should be suppressed to prevent this sort of tracking.

Storing data with JavaScript: Mechanisms designed for JavaScript to store data include the not-yet-standard "web storage" (or "DOM storage") features already implemented in some browsers. Like HTTP cookies, these mechanisms of persistent storage have been designed specifically for storing potentially identifying information, so browsers providing this feature will also provide options for controlling which data are stored.

Storage in `window.name`: Each window object in the document object model (a set of objects presented to JavaScript software running in a web browser) has a "name" attribute, readable and writeable by JavaScript. It was designed to give the window a name by which to refer to it. The window retains its name until a script changes it again or until the window is closed. Because this feature was not designed for tracking users, there are no privacy controls designed with it. This property can be used to track users within a browsing session, and even works between domains (e.g. secretmail.com could set window.name, for it to be read by tracking.com). Note that this mechanism does not allow tracking between browsing sessions, and of course it does not work for browsers not running JavaScript. On its own, in fact, `window.name` is not very useful, but it was deemed useful enough by the author of the *Evercookie*, a JavaScript library to use many different techniques (including many in this section) to track users in a very difficult to circumvent manner [40].

Storing data with plug-ins: Many web browser plug-ins designed for "rich internet applications" also provide rich tracking features. Adobe Flash [38] and Microsoft Silverlight [23] both have features for storing data locally on clients' computers. Because these plug-ins are distributed and managed separately from web browsers, instructing a web browser to clear its cache and cookie storage is not necessary enough to ensure privacy. This is starting to change: some web browsers have been updated to clear such plug-ins' storage.

Using browser history: The methods discussed so far have been concerned with tracking a user over one website, or at least with co-operating websites. However, there are also mechanisms by which a website can discover which other sites a user has visited.

The first is the `Referrer` header. This HTTP header is sent from the browser to the server and contains the URL of the page that the user navigated away from. Although the scope for using this is limited, it can still reveal to the owner of a page how a user found that page. For example, if a user were to follow a link from http://bbs.example/embarrassing-post/ to http://marketing.example/, the owner of marketing example would be able to see that the user came from http://bbs.example/embarrassing-post/. The HTTP specification recommends that web browsers have an option to prevent sending the Referer header (RFC 2616, § 15.1.3) for this reason.

The cascading style sheets (CSS) standard—a language for specifying layout and formatting properties for HTML pages—specifies a way to apply properties to links conditionally, based on whether the user has visited the link target. This allows websites to probe the user's history one URL at a time to discover whether the user has visited certain sites. One way to do this is to set visited links to use a much larger font size than unvisited links. JavaScript software can then obtain the size of the link, or positions of elements around it, to discover whether the link target has been visited.

Another way, one that does not require JavaScript, is to set visited links to have a background image. The server can then find out that the link target has been visited when it receives a request for the image. In March 2010, it was reported that modifications had been made to the popular web browser Firefox to prevent "history sniffing", as it is called [63].

It may also be possible to analyse a browser's history by timing how long it takes to load resources [29]. If a user has visited a web page before, elements of the page may have been cached, so retrieving them will take less time than otherwise.

It is much easier for "little brother" to look at browser history, since he has physical access to the computer and is probably able to just open the web browser and look at the browsing history.

Fingerprinting: Almost all web browsers send some form of identifying information in the headers of each request they send.

- The `User-Agent` header contains a string identifying the name of the user agent (browser), its version and other information.
- The `Accept` header communicates which media types the browser will accept.
- The `Accept-Charset` and `Accept-Encoding` headers determine which transfer encodings (compression, for example) and character sets are accepted.
- The `Accept-Language` header reveals which human languages the browser will accept.

These headers can be combined to provide at least 18.8 bits of identifying information [24].

There are various web browser add-ons, such as *NoScript* and *Ghostery*, designed to defend against many of the above techniques by not running JavaScript until requested by the user, detecting privacy problems in web pages and blocking cookies. Such add-ons were listed in a report from the European project *PrimeLife*, with an analysis of how often the tracking techniques are used on the web [22].

Facebook "like" and other buttons: Recently, social networking websites such as *Myspace* and *Facebook* have collected a vast quantity of interlinked information about millions of people. Facebook's creator, Mark Zuckerberg, claims "people have really gotten comfortable not only sharing more information and different kinds, but also more openly and with more people. That social norm is just something that has evolved over time [39]". This amount of valuable information can be used by burglars [18], tax collectors [61], employers [58], advertisers and law enforcement in criminal investigations. Facebook's using facial recognition software gives this information even more worth.

Facebook's "like" button has allowed it to track users even on other websites. The "like" button, along with other buttons belonging to *Reddit* and *Digg*, can be added by website owners to their pages. Facebook encourages websites of all descriptions to include the code for their button on their pages. The idea is that a user visiting a non-Facebook page can indicate to their Facebook friends that they like the page by clicking on the button. The Facebook button instructs Facebook to record that the user has clicked on it. This fact is then given to the user's "friends". The popularity of this sort of "widget" is immense. The software quality management consultancy Q-Success has measured that 21 % of websites use these widgets [57].

The privacy problem is that these widgets are included in web pages by including JavaScript software directly from the social website. Merely visiting a page with a Facebook "like" button causes the button to be loaded, and that notifies Facebook. If the user is logged onto Facebook, the notification is accompanied by the user's Facebook cookie. So Facebook knows the pages you visit, whether you "like" them or not [28]. Moreover, the software could have the power to follow every movement of the mouse cursor within the browser window and can send this information to the social website by means of an *iframe* element or image request, along with the social site's cookies. The pervasiveness of social widgets allows social websites to track people across many different web pages, even if they have logged into none of them.

2.3.2.2 Person-to-Person Communication: e-Mail

As our second case study, we look at e-mail, which is the predominant form of person-to-person communication. E-mail already existed in a primitive form in 1973, when security and privacy were not concerns. As e-mail has changed and become more complicated, features have been added on haphazardly, and many of the features have (in the interests of functionality) made security and privacy worse.

E-mail typically travels in several "legs" of the journey from sender to recipient. The first leg is from the sender's mail browser (or "mail user agent", MUA) to her service provider. This leg is typically encrypted using a key based on the service provider's public key. Next, in another leg the message is sent from the sender's service provider to the receiver's service provider. This step is usually not encrypted; in brief, it is encrypted only if both service providers support the STARTTLS protocol. It is difficult for users to determine, for a given message, whether that will be the case; moreover, a man-in-the-middle attacker can perform a downgrade attack, by removing the STARTTLS announcement. The last leg occurs when the receiver downloads his mail from his service provider. This step is typically encrypted using a key established using the public key of the receiver's service provider.

In spite of the fact that two of the three legs are typically encrypted, and sometimes all three are, the arrangement gives plenty of opportunity for brothers of all sizes to access a user's e-mail (see Table 2.1). The sender's and receiver's service provider (middle brother) process the e-mail messages in the clear, and have the opportunity to profile the user on the basis of what she sends and receives. As has been confirmed by the Snowden revelations of 2013, the service providers also allow intelligence agencies (big brother) direct access too. Additionally, since client mail software typically stores messages on the computer's hard disk in the clear, family members, computer repair shops, cleaning staff and of course malware on the user's computer can potentially have access too.

Features that have been added to e-mail over the years can make the security and privacy aspects even worse. Some e-mail messages are in HTML format, which can link to images on remote servers. These images can be hidden by virtue of being very small (just one pixel), and the same colour as the message's background. The image URL can point to the sender's server and can contain a unique identifier, so that when the image is loaded by the recipient's mail reader, the sender is informed that the message has been opened. These images are called *tracking pixels*, and are useful for spammers ("middle brother", "opportunistic") or just to see whether a friend has read a message ("little brother", "opportunistic"). Tracking pixels can easily be defeated if mail clients refuse to fetch external resources until requested by the user, which most now do.

End-to-end encryption: End-to-end encryption is when a message is encrypted by its sender with the recipients' public keys and remains encrypted until it is decrypted by one of the recipients. Obviously, this is much better than the piecemeal encryption described in the previous section, where each leg was encrypted with the keys established and held by the intermediate servers. Two common standards for end-to-end-encrypted e-mail are *OpenPGP* (RFC 4880) and *S/MIME* (RFC 3851). They both require the user's software to store their private key, and differ mainly in the way they verify who owns which public key.

S/MIME (secure MIME) was designed in 1995 as an extension of the MIME format—the standard for e-mail attachments—and uses certificate authorities to issue certificates (signatures) on users' public keys. A certificate authority must be trusted by both the sender and the receiver of e-mail. This works well for internal mail within a large company, because the company can act as its own CA. For external mail, for smaller organisations and for individuals, a third-party CA needs to be used, and that often requires payment.

Some certificate authorities such as *Comodo* offer certificates for free to individuals, but insist on generating the key pair themselves. This is particularly insecure because a compromised or malicious certificate authority can then retain a copy of all the users' private keys, which, with the co-operation of an e-mail service (perhaps under threat of violence by the state), can be used to decrypt mail.

Most CAs do not generate the private key; the user does that, and sends only the public key to be certified. This prevents CAs from launching "passive" attacks. But they can still launch active attacks by issuing a false certificate for the user, based on the CA's own choice of private key. This attack relies on being able to capture the encrypted e-mail, so could be launched in cooperation with ISPs.

The core problem with CAs is that they have to be trusted by the sender and the receiver. This problem is made worse by the fact that there are typically multiple (perhaps hundreds) of CAs installed in e-mail browsers (and web browsers), *and any CA can certify any key*. That means that a single malicious CA can launch fake-key attacks on any e-mail address, not just the ones the user had in mind when they accepted to use that CA.

Ideally, mail software will automatically find S/MIME certificates; sometimes, large organisations have a server set up for this purpose. For example, Boeing hosts an LDAP server with certificates.[1] *OpenPGP* is more flexible than S/MIME. It is targeted at individual users, so it aims to remove the need of certificate authorities. In OpenPGP, each public key can be signed by several people who have met the key's owner and verified that they do indeed own the key. In this way, S/MIME's hierarchical structure is replaced by a *web of trust*, reflecting the social network. A user can decide to trust a public key by verifying a signature by a key they already trust.

As an example, suppose Alice wants to send a message to Bob. She needs to know his public key. She already has Charlie's public key, perhaps because he gave it to her when they met, and Charlie has signed a certificate for Bob's public key. That is some evidence, but not quite enough, because she does not know Charlie very well and is not sure if she can trust him. ("Trusting" Charlie means being sure that he has no malicious intent, and that he is competent enough to judge whether the given key is Bob's.) Fortunately, as well as Charlie, there is Dave, Eliza and Frederica. Alice has all their public keys already, and they have also signed Bob's key. Each one of them provides further evidence of the authenticity of that key. Combining the evidence, Alice is assured that the given public key is Bob's.

This decentralised web of trust requires users to verify their friends' public keys, which is probably one reason for its lack of adoption. Existing software is also not good at finding long paths through the web of trust. For example, in the case where Alice signed Bob's key, Bob signed Charlie's, Charlie signed Dennis's and Dennis signed Edward's, Alice would have a difficult time verifying Edward's key: existing software cannot find the path from Alice's key, through Bob's, Charlie's and Dennis's, unless Alice had already verified and imported all those keys.

Although they each take very different approaches to public key management, neither S/MIME nor OpenPGP manage to hide the details from users, and as a

---

[1] Web interface at http://www.boeingsuppliers.com/ldap_proxy/get_cert.html.

consequence neither has been widely adopted in comparison to TLS, which hides most of the details (users do not even need to know what public and private keys are) and is used very frequently on the web. S/MIME and OpenPGP also share some other problems: managing keys and e-mail from multiple devices requires the user to manage their private keys themself; mail servers cannot perform functions that are now expected: mail filtering, spam filtering and searching; and e-mail metadata, including the sender, the recipient and the subject line, are not kept secret.

2.3.3 Content and Metadata

The distinction between content (messages, pictures, voice) and metadata (times, addresses, physical location, bandwidth usage) is politically significant: for example, the Draft Communications Data Bill differentiates between "communications data" and "content", and allows the collection of the former but not the latter. Communication content, which could be unstructured text, voice or video, is less suitable for automated analysis than the metadata. It is much easier to automatically extract meaningful information from metadata, which already have structure, than from text, voice or video, which would require natural language processing, image recognition and other difficult and unreliable techniques. Furthermore, although metadata about one telephone call (the date and time of the call, the duration, the dialler and the receiver) may seem innocuous, combining a vast collection of such data can be far more useful than is intuitive [15].

HM Revenue and Customs uses surveillance to investigate tax fraud. This often involves looking at "communications data" (which includes the source and destination of messages, but not the messages' contents), which happened over 14,000 times in 2011 [37]. More intrusive, covert surveillance was authorised 172 times between October 2011 and September 2012.

While TLS, S/MIME or OpenPGP can protect content, they cannot protect the communications data: the senders' and recipients' e-mail addresses. Protecting that seems to be much harder.

The onion router, *Tor*, is a system that can protect some metadata on the internet. In particular, a user can hide their IP address, network location and geographic location. Tor does this by moving packets around a random route, and using layers of encryption to hide the whole route, so that each point in the route only knows the previous point and the next point. In theory, all the points in the route have to be compromised for the anonymity to be broken (there exist some timing attacks against Tor which avoid the need to compromise the whole route), and a new route is chosen every 10 min.

Because of the long routes used, and the high number of users compared to the number of Tor relays, using Tor is often a slow and inconsistent experience, which makes it unsuitable for everyday use.

2.4 The Future

2.4.1 Our Vision

The bleak picture of the preceding sections indicates that privacy in our everyday lives is threatened by technology in many ways. There is a real possibility that humans would not have any form of privacy in the future. It is not easy to see what can be done about this. The privacy enhancing technologies discussed (such as TLS and OpenPGP) are a good start, but we need to rethink privacy from the bottom up in order to build it into our computer systems. Privacy needs to be a major part of systems from the beginning because it affects all aspects of how the systems work. Adding privacy afterwards tends to require compromises.

We should also look carefully at why privacy is threatened. Although privacy is considered broadly desirable, it can be used to hide illegal or immoral behaviour. Privacy should be overridden in some cases, such as some criminal investigations. Humans live together in a society, and this implies that they are to some extent accountable to each other. For example, we accept that our bags and pockets are searched at airports, and we accept the duty of declaring our income to tax officials. These actions invade our privacy, but they are supposed to be for the good of society as a whole.

This indicates that a balance between privacy and accountability is needed. For example, we may choose to accommodate targeted and properly authorised criminal investigations while preventing mass-surveillance and data mining.

The technologies we currently use for privacy with computer systems either protect everything or nothing. E-mail messages are either completely encrypted or sent in the clear. Connections are either completely private between two computers or are unencrypted. Unlike these traditional systems, a balance could be provided in which privacy holds in general, but may be overridden in specific user-verifiable conditions. A simple example might be that e-mail is being kept private, but be released to the police if a relevant search warrant is issued. But this should be done in such a way that the conditions, and whether or not they have been used to override privacy, can be verified by whomever the information is about.

2.4.2 Achieving Privacy, Security, and Accountability

It appears to be impossible to codify precisely the circumstances in which law enforcement agencies should be considered entitled to access the data stored in the logs created by usage of mobile phones, the internet, payment systems and transport systems. One could instead try to frame legislation in terms of quantities of information; the law enforcement agencies may access a specified proportion of information about an individual, an event or during a period.

But stipulating such proportions is unlikely to be satisfactory, either from the citizen's point of view or that of the law enforcers. A third possibility is to rely on judges and other trusted parties to consider requests, one by one. This is roughly what happened up until the aftermath of the September 2001 attacks; since then, as the Snowden revelations have shown, law enforcers have obtained much broader permissions to undertake surveillance. The approach using judges to consider requests one by one does not scale up well; more and more information is being created, and therefore there is an ever-increasing set of opportunities for it to be used, or abused.

The approach we suggest is to supplement the procedural checks-and-balances with verifiable and quantitative accountability that allows citizens to understand how much surveillance is being carried out. Under the proposal, there would still be legislation and procedures for determining whether access is allowed, on a case-by-case basis; but it would be supported by quantitative information about actual access that took place, against which citizens can hold politicians accountable. We provide a means for individuals and society as a whole to obtain verifiable evidence about what the degree and nature of the surveillance that has taken place, and to vote for governments and officers that demonstrate proportionality in the way they use the data.

"Verifiable evidence" means that citizens have a means to check the veracity of the levels of surveillance that are reported. This is achieved using cryptographic protocols that produce data which can be subjected to tests by citizens. In principle, any citizen can verify the data, although it might be technically difficult and/or expensive to do so. It is sufficient if some trustworthy organisations (such as universities, charities, or journalists) do so on behalf of everyone else.

Example: mobile phones: Under our proposal, security agencies would be able to access mobile phone records according to agreed rules, roughly as now. This includes discovering about a suspect who he phoned or texted, or received calls or texts from, as well as where he went (since mobile phone operators also store location information), at what time, and so on. However, the accesses made in this way are logged in a way which cannot be avoided or faked. Any individual can obtain verifiable information from the logs about the accesses made. The granularity of such information can be determined in a way that appropriately balances privacy and security; for example, it is unlikely that it would be appropriate for individuals to obtain information about surveillance accesses concerning themselves in real-time, since such information may alert criminals to the fact that they are being investigated. Information concerning data accesses about oneself may therefore be made available only after a certain period of time, perhaps 2 years. But coarser-grained information about what proportion of each day's records is accessed across a city or country might be made available immediately. In this way, citizens can hold the authorities and the government accountable for surveillance accesses.

Putting this idea into practice involves solving numerous technical challenges. There must be unavoidable mechanisms for ensuring that the surveillance accesses are logged, and that the logs cannot be erased or modified. There needs to be mechanism for citizens to access the logs; as mentioned, this access might be mediated, in order to limit the granularity of the information that can be seen. Finally, we need a mechanism to allow citizens to obtain proofs that the information they are given about surveillance accesses is correct.

Developing these ideas is ongoing research; the details are likely to be different for different applications. The mobile phone application is likely to be one of the most challenging, because the technology and the use-cases are already very complex. In the following section, we propose a framework for a more straightforward example, that of wireless ticketing systems.

2.4.3 Example: Wireless Tickets

Wireless ticket systems (such as the London Oyster card or the Paris Navigo card) allow passengers to travel on city-wide transport by presenting a contactless smartcard at the time of taking a journey. The traditional paper-ticket system that preceded it allowed perfectly anonymous travel, but the wireless card has made transport ticketing into a classical privacy-invasive technology. With a wireless ticket, a passenger's journeys are logged and stored in perpetuity. To combat terrorism, and to avoid the need to obtain court orders each time, the UK intelligence agencies MI5 and MI6 have sought full automated access to Transport for London's Oyster smart card database. The data could potentially be used not just for law enforcement but potentially for advertising purposes, or even criminal stalking and harassment.

We briefly outline some ideas for making accountable the accesses to the wireless ticketing database. Assume *pk* is a public key belonging to a *decrypting party* (DP). The entity DP can be a TPM-attested service, or can be distributed as several independent parties where we assume that at least one of them is honest. We consider these ways to securely implement DP in more detail later; for now, we assume DP is a trusted party.

This data may be produced directly by the wireless ticket, and transmitted encrypted to the reader installed at the transport station. Under this arrangement, the reader informs the wireless ticket about the name of the station and the current time. The wireless card appends the information about the user identity, and encrypts the whole with *pk* before sending the encrypted packet back to the reader. Thus, the information is held in a database, encrypted by *pk*.

The core idea is that DP will decrypt any part of the data requested by the authorities, but will create a log of all the decryptions it performs. The passenger may inspect the log, perhaps after a time interval, and perhaps mediated by an access control system, to verify how much of the information about her has been decrypted.

2.4.3.1 Collecting and Querying the Data

We suppose that the system creates records detailing the entrances and exits from the transport system. For example, if Alice starts a journey at Knightsbridge at 09:31 on 2 March 2013, the ticketing system creates an entry

$$\{\text{Alice, Knightsbridge, entry, 20130302, } 09:31\}_{pk}$$

We suppose this data is encrypted by Alice's smart card, using the public key pk, of which the secret key is known only to DP.

Queries: The authorities can choose which parts of the data they want to access. For example, if Alice is a suspect, they can request that DP decrypts all records containing Alice in the database. They can stipulate further conditions about the other fields (location, activity, date and time) too. DP performs the necessary decryptions and creates an entry in the log of accesses.

2.4.3.2 How the Log Works

The log is a verifiably append-only record of all the decryptions that have taken place. The log is designed such that nothing can be removed from it without the removal being noticed by everyone. This allows citizens to be certain that no decryption can take place without being forever evident in the log. Methods such as those that implement the log of certificate transparency [43, 60] can be used. They allow a log maintainer (who does not have to be trusted) to update the log in a way that any observer can verify is append-only, and to produce proofs of presence or absence of data in the log.

2.4.3.3 Citizens' Access to the Logs

On the assumption that DP acts correctly, the logs provide complete information about all the data accesses that were made for surveillance purposes. However, as mentioned, it might not be desirable to allow citizens to have immediate and direct access to the logs; for example, this could alert criminals to the fact of an investigation concerning them. We envisage there being rules, decided democratically, for what sort of access to the logs is allowed. In the case of the wireless ticketing system, we can imagine a spectrum starting with a version that is "generous" to the citizen, by providing maximal access, with various degrees of generosity and ending with a rather "mean" version:

- The generous version gives a full account, for a given individual, of all the accesses to their journey data that have taken place.
- An intermediate version gives a time-delayed and quantitative account, but it lacks detail. For example, the individual gets to read the proportion of journeys whose data has been accessed that have taken place more than, say, 2 years ago.

- A mean version gives a real-time but much coarser view. An individual can read the proportion of accesses made for all journeys taken by everyone, but cannot see which accesses are about her.

2.4.3.4   Implementing DP

The job of the decrypting party DP is very simple and fully automatable. DP is not required to make any judgments about whether access should be allowed; it blindly decrypts every authorised request. However, DP is required to insert every decryption into the log, and therefore the system relies on the trustworthiness of DP. There are several ways in which this trustworthiness can be assured.

The most promising method is to distribute DP across several parties, in such a way that the system is secure provided that at least one of the parties is honest. Each party making up DP holds part of the decryption key, and performs part of the decryption. Each party must also insert information about the decryption into the log. If any party does not do so, it is exposed as possibly dishonest.

Another method is to use trusted computing hardware, such as the Trusted Platform Module (TPM [34]), ARM's TrustZone [46], or Intel's SGX [49]. The idea is that the key pk under which the data is held encrypted can be verifiably bound to particular code base which encodes the behaviour of DP. At the time, the key is created by the trusted computing hardware; the hardware associates it with register values which represent a secure hash of the binary of DP. This information is exposed to arbitrary observers: anyone can verify that the key pk was indeed produced by trustworthy hardware, and is bound to the binary of DP. The fact that the secure hardware only allows DP to decrypt the data ensures that the data can be processed only in accordance with DP. Note that DP has to be fully automatic for this to work. Note also that the trustworthy hardware must provide facilities that prevent roll-back attacks, in which DP is presented with an out-of-date version of the log.

These two methods can be combined together. If DP is a set of parties, one or more of them can choose to perform its role using trustworthy hardware.

Cryptographically more sophisticated implementations using fully homomorphic encryption [32] or functional encryption [16] may also be possible.

2.4.3.5   Conclusion

This chapter set out the idea that surveillance could be made accountable to citizens, in such a way that people could decide through the democratic process how much and what kind of surveillance they want to allow. Moreover, the quantity and nature of the surveillance is *verifiable* by citizens; rather than merely having to believe statements about it, they obtain proof that the statements are correct.

Key escrow schemes have been discussed before. In 1998 [9], cryptographer Bruce Schneier concluded that "key recovery systems are inherently less secure, more costly, and more difficult to use than similar systems without a recovery feature." With today's much greater computing power, and with the invention of the TPM, it may be possible to compensate for the concerns expressed in 1998.

We only scratch the surface. There is still a vast amount to do, to refine the ideas and propose mechanisms for realising them. The problem that these ideas address can only get much worse over the coming decades, as the internet of things generates vastly more data about our lives than before, and more and more ways emerge to use the data in privacy invasive ways.

We conclude that privacy is very difficult to get right, with even the most seemingly innocuous protocol feature may allow tracking, surveillance or spying. There are also multiple levels at which privacy on the internet can be lost: metadata about connections is almost always unprotected, TLS's certificate checking can be vulnerable, and documents and messages might have names and private information accidentally left in them. It will get much worse as we move towards a world of big data and ubiquitous, pervasive computers and the internet of things. We propose cryptographic systems that provide a balance of privacy and accountability as the way forward, since the current system of insecure protocols and unaccountable surveillance provides neither properly.

References

1. Monkey brains control robot arms. (2003). BBC. http://news.bbc.co.uk/1/hi/health/3186850.stm.
2. Sony recalls copy-protected CDs. (2005). BBC. http://news.bbc.co.uk/1/hi/technology/4441928.stm.
3. Chaos computer club analyzes government malware. (2011). http://www.ccc.de/en/updates/2011/staatstrojaner.
4. Facebook sorry over face tagging launch. (2011). BBC. http://www.bbc.co.uk/news/technology-13693791.
5. Germany spyware: Minister calls for probe of state use. (2011). BBC. http://www.bbc.co.uk/news/world-europe-15253259.
6. NSA slides explain the PRISM data-collection program. (2013). The Washington Post. http://www.washingtonpost.com/wp-srv/special/politics/prism-collection-documents/.
7. Live Q&A with Edward Snowden. (2014). http://www.freesnowden.is/asksnowden.html.
8. The NSA files. (2014). The guardian. http://www.theguardian.com/world/the-nsa-files.
9. Abelson, H., Anderson, R., Bellovin, S. M., Benaloh, J., Blaze, M., Diffie, W., Gilmore, J., Neumann, P. G., Rivest, R. L., Schiller, J. I., & Schneier B. (1998). The risks of key recovery, key escrow, and trusted third-party encryption. http://www.schneier.com/paper-key-escrow.html.
10. Acquisti, A., Gross, R., & Stutzman, F. (2011). Faces of Facebook: Privacy in the age of augmented reality. BlackHat USA. http://www.heinz.cmu.edu/acquisti/face-recognition-study-FAQ/acquisti-faces-BLACKHAT-draft.pdf.
11. Arapinis, M, Borgaonkar, R., Golde, N., Mancini, L., Redon, K., Ritter, E., & Ryan, M. (2012). New privacy issues in mobile telephony: fix and verification. In *ACM Conference on Computer and Communications Security* (pp. 205–216). http://www.cs.bham.ac.uk/mdr/research/papers/pdf/12-UMTS.pdf.
12. Bamford, J. (2012). The NSA is building the country's biggest spy center. Wired magazine. http://www.wired.com/threatlevel/2012/03/ff_nsadatacenter/all/1.
13. Black, J. (2001). Don't make privacy the next victim of terror. Bloomberg Businessweek. http://www.businessweek.com/bwdaily/dnflash/oct2001/nf20011104_7412.htm, 2001.

14. Blaze, M. (1994). Protocol failure in the escrowed encryption standard. In *Proceedings of the Second ACM Conference on Computer and Communications Security (CCS)*. http://www.crypto.com/papers/.
15. Blaze, M. (2013). Phew, NSA is just collecting metadata. (you should still worry.). Wired magazine. http://www.wired.com/opinion/2013/06/phew-it-was-just-metadata-not-think-again/.
16. Boneh, D., Sahai, A., Waters, B. Functional encryption: Definitions and challenges. In *Theory of Cryptography* (pp. 253—273). Springer.
17. Bosker, B. (2011). Facebook's Randi Zuckerberg: Anonymity online "has to go away". Huffington Post. http://www.huffingtonpost.com/2011/07/27/randi-zuckerberg-anonymity-online_n_910892.html.
18. Britten, N. (2010). Facebook users warned of burglary risk. The Telegraph. http://www.telegraph.co.uk/technology/facebook/8004716/Facebook-users-warned-of-burglary-risk.html.
19. Carrier iQ, Inc. What data is collected? http://www.carrieriq.com/what-data-is-collected/.
20. Chothia, T., & Smirnov, V. (2010). A traceability attack against e-passports. In *Proceedings of the 14th International Conference on Financial Cryptography and Data Security*. http://www.cs.bham.ac.uk/tpc/Papers/PassportTrace.pdf.
21. Clayton, R. The Phorm "Webwise" system. http://www.cl.cam.ac.uk/rnc1/080518-phorm.pdf.
22. PrimeLife Consortium. (2011). Privacy-enhancing browser extensions. http://www.w3.org/2011/D1.2.3/.
23. Microsoft Corporation. Application storage. http://www.microsoft.com/getsilverlight/resources/documentation/AppStorage.aspx.
24. Eckersley, P. (2010). How unique is your web browser? In *Proceedings of the Privacy Enhancing Technologies Symposium (PETS 2010)*, volume 6205 of *Lecture Notes in Computer Science*. Springer. http://panopticlick.eff.org/browser-uniqueness.pdf.
25. Trevor Eckhart. CarrierIQ part 2. androidsecuritytest.com/features/logs-and-services/loggers/carrieriq/carrieriq-part2/.
26. Espiner, T. (2012). ISPs kept in dark about UK's plans to intercept Twitter. http://www.zdnet.co.uk/news/security-threats/2012/02/20/isps-kept-in-dark-about-uks-plans-to-intercept-twitter-40095083/.
27. Inc. Facebook. Data use policy. https://www.facebook.com/about/privacy/your-info.
28. Inc. Facebook. (2013). What information does Facebook get when i visit a site with the like button or another social plugin? https://www.facebook.com/help/186325668085084.
29. Felten, E. W., Schneider, M. A. (2000). Timing attacks on web privacy. In *ACM Conference on Computer and Communications Security*, pp. 25–32.
30. Electronic Frontier Foundation. Sony BMG settlement FAQ. https://w2.eff.org/IP/DRM/Sony-BMG/settlement_faq.php.
31. Gahran, A. (2010). Using Wi-Fi? Firesheep may endanger your security. CNN. http://edition.cnn.com/2010/TECH/mobile/11/01/firesheep.wifi.security/index.html.
32. Gentry, C. (2009). *A Fully Homomorphic Encryption Scheme*. PhD thesis, Stanford University, Advisor Dan Boneh.
33. Miniwatts Marketing Group. (2012). World internet users and population stats. http://www.internetworldstats.com/stats.htm.
34. Trusted Computing Group. (2007). *TPM Main Specification*.
35. Hinsliff, G. (2008). MI5 seeks powers to trawl records in new terror hunt. The Observer. http://www.guardian.co.uk/uk/2008/mar/16/uksecurity.terrorism.
36. The White House. (1994). Statement of the press secretary. http://epic.org/crypto/clipper/white_house_statement_2_94.html.
37. Huber, N. (2013). The tax man is watching you: (HMRC) snoops on public 14,000 times in a year. The Independent. http://www.independent.co.uk/news/uk/home-news/the-tax-man-is-watching-you-hmrc-snoops-on-public-14000-times-in-a-year-8449862.html.
38. Adobe Systems Incorporated. What are local shared objects? http://www.adobe.com/products/flashplayer/articles/lso/.

39. Johnson, B. (2010). Privacy no longer a social norm, says Facebook founder. Guardian. http://www.guardian.co.uk/technology/2010/jan/11/facebook-privacy.
40. Kamkar, S. Evercookie—virtually irrevocable persistent cookies. http://samy.pl/evercookie/.
41. Keneally, M. (2013). Yahoo CEO Marissa Mayer feared being sent to jail for treason over NSA scandal. Daily Mail. http://www.dailymail.co.uk/news/article-2419441/Yahoo-CEO-Marissa-Mayer-feared-sent-jail-treason-NSA-scandal.html.
42. LaPlante, M. D. Spies like us: NSA to build huge facility in Utah. The Salt Lake Tribune. http://www.sltrib.com/ci_12735293.
43. Laurie, B., Langley, A., & Kasper, E. (2013). Certificate transparency. http://tools.ietf.org/html/rfc6962.
44. Lewis, P. (2008). Fears over privacy as police expand surveillance project. The Guardian. http://www.guardian.co.uk/uk/2008/sep/15/civilliberties.police.
45. Lewis, P., & Vallée, M. (2009). Revealed: police databank on thousands of protesters. http://www.guardian.co.uk/uk/2009/mar/06/police-surveillance-protesters-journalists-climate-kingsnorth?INTCMP=ILCNETTXT3487.
46. ARM Limited. (2009). *ARM TrustZone API Specification, version 3.0.*
47. Path Intelligence Ltd. Revolutionary technology for detailed data insights. http://www.pathintelligence.com/technology/.
48. Martin, R. (2005). Mind control. Wired magazine. http://www.wired.com/wired/archive/13.03/brain.html.
49. McKeen, F., Alexandrovich, I., Berenzon, A., Rozas, C., Shafi, H., Shanbhogue, V., & Savagaonkar, U. Innovative instructions and software model for isolated execution. In *Second Workshop on Hardware and Architectural Support for Security and Privacy (HASP 2013)*.
50. Mitchell, S. Anger over mass web surveillance plans. PC Pro magazine. http://www.pcpro.co.uk/news/security/372985/anger-over-mass-web-surveillance-plans.
51. Nightingale, J. (2011). Fraudulent *.google.com certificate. Mozilla Security Blog. https://blog.mozilla.org/security/2011/08/29/fraudulent-google-com-certificate/.
52. The Home Office. (2010). Communications data. http://www.homeoffice.gov.uk/counter-terrorism/communications-data/.
53. Page, L. (2008). Spooks want to go fishing in Oyster database. The Register. http://www.theregister.co.uk/2008/03/17/spooks_want_oyster/.
54. Pegoraro, R. (2011). Google's Eric Schmidt steps down, depriving web of future quotes. Washington Post. http://www.washingtonpost.com/wp-dyn/content/article/2011/01/20/AR2011012006128.html.
55. Perlroth, N. (2013). NSA able to foil basic safeguards of privacy on web. The New York Times. http://www.nytimes.com/2013/09/06/us/nsa-foils-much-internet-encryption.html.
56. Poulsen, K. (2007). FBI's secret spyware tracks down teen who made bomb threats. Wired magazine. http://www.wired.com/politics/law/news/2007/07/fbi_spyware?currentPage=all.
57. Q-Success. W3Techs web technology surveys. http://w3techs.com/technologies/overview/social_widget/all.
58. Ben Quinn. (2008). Virgin sacks 13 over Facebook "chav" remarks. The Guardian. http://www.guardian.co.uk/business/2008/nov/01/virgin-atlantic-facebook.
59. RIsen, J., Lichtblau, E. (2005). Bush lets U.S. spy on callers without courts. The New York Times. http://www.nytimes.com/2005/12/16/politics/16program.html?pagewanted=1_r=1.
60. Ryan, M. (2014). Enhanced certificate transparency and end-to-end encrypted mail. In *Network and Distributed System Security (NDSS)*. http://www.cs.bham.ac.uk/mdr/research/papers/pdf/14-ndss-cert.pdf.
61. Saunders, L. (2009). Is "friending" in your future? Better pay your taxes first. The Wall Street Journal. http://online.wsj.com/article/SB125132627009861985.html.
62. Schneier, B. (2010). Anonymity and the internet. https://www.schneier.com/blog/archives/2010/02/anonymity_and_t_3.html, 2010.
63. Sid Stamm. Plugging the CSS history leak. http://blog.mozilla.com/security/2010/03/31/plugging-the-css-history-leak/.

64. Story, L. (2008). A company promises the deepest data mining yet. The New York Times. http://www.nytimes.com/2008/03/20/business/media/20adcoside.html.
65. Sullivan, B. (2001). FBI software cracks encryption wall. MSNBC. http://www.msnbc.msn.com/id/3341694/ns/technology_and_science-security/t/fbi-software-cracks-encryption-wall/.